# Amillennialism

# Today

By

William E. Cox

REFORMED PUBLISHING CO.
g, New Jersey
1980

ISBN: 0-87552-151-7


Library of Congress Catalogue Card Number 66-28450
Printed in the United States of America

# Amillennialism

# Today

# INTRODUCTION

Amillennialists have been accused of expending most of their energies criticizing other millennial theories, while they themselves have no positive system of theological beliefs. Even though these charges come from those who hold postmillennial or premillennial views, they still set forth a need for a statement of those things most surely believed among amillennialists.

In our examination of amillennialism we shall deal somewhat with the history of this movement, some of its outstanding leaders, and its cardinal beliefs. In the latter category it will be necessary to settle for a majority view of their beliefs, since not every exponent of amillennialism would agree on every point of Scripture. Nor do they even attempt a forced conformity as a basis of fellowship.

Amillennialism oversteps denominational lines; in fact, it oversteps theological lines. Men who agree on what the Bible has to say, or does not have to say, with reference to the millennium may stand poles apart on other cardinal doctrines of the Bible. Some of these differences will be enumerated later. What we are dealing with here is cardinal beliefs of amillennialism, and not cardinal doctrines of the entire Bible.

Some premillenarian writers claim unanimity for their group while casting aspersions on the differences of opinion among other schools of thought. Actually, more pronounced differences exist among premillenarians than among any of the other schools. Have these writers never heard of schisms in their ranks growing out of the four different opinions concerning the rapture? They divide up into pretribulation rapturists, midtribulation rapturists, postribulation rapturists, and partial tribulation rapturists. And when will the Old Testament saints be resurrected? Many different answers to this question would be forthcoming, depending on which particular premillenarian one might be talking with. Premillenarians have in their ranks — and this is also true of postmillenarians and amillenarians

— immersionists and pedobaptists, covenant theologians and anti-covenant theologians, Calvinists and Arminians, those who believe in eternal security and those who despise this belief with a vengeance. There are in fact three distinct schools of premillenarians — the futurist, the dispensationalist, and the historic premillenarians.* Many historic premillenarians have no place in their theology for a separate future for the Jew, while this doctrine makes up the entire framework of dispensationalism. Many premillenarians (the futurists) believe Israel will have a separate destiny from that of the church, yet do not believe time is packaged in seven dispensations. So that, while these three schools agree that Christ will come before (pre) the millennium, they differ sharply on many other doctrines.

It can easily be seen, then, that amillenarians are not alone in having differences among themselves. I am reminded of the story of the Baptist church which was having a summer slump in attendance. According to the story, the minister looked out the window and sighed, "Well, thank goodness the Methodists are not doing any better."

After this rather negative introduction let us proceed now to an examination of amillennialism.

All Scripture quotations, unless otherwise noted, will be from the American Standard Version, published in 1901.

---

*William E. Cox, *Biblical Studies in Final Things*, deals with five millennial theories.

# CONTENTS

# I

## AMILLENNIALISM DEFINED

What exactly is amillennialism? What is the biblical basis for this belief? And how does this school of thought differ from other schools of millennial thought? Before answering these questions it seems wise to state some things which amillennialism is not.

First of all, amillenarians do not deny the existence of a millennium. They believe explicitly in the millennium of Revelation 20. They simply interpret the passage differently than do other millennialists. More will be said on this interpretation later.

The term "amillennial" is an unfortunate one in one sense of the word, because it literally means "no millennium." The label has been made into a libel in many cases. Unwary laymen look up Webster's meaning and conclude that the amillenarian discards the teaching of Revelation 20. Yet, a more suitable term has not been found to describe amillennialism so as to distinguish it from premillennialism and postmillennialism. Some have suggested the name "realized millennialism." This writer prefers the term "biblical millennialism."

A good definition of amillennialism comes from the pen of one of its severest critics. "Its most general character is that of denial of a *literal* reign of Christ upon the earth. Satan is conceived as bound at the first coming of Christ. The present age between the first and second comings is the fulfillment of the millennium. Its adherents are divided on whether the millennium is being fulfilled now on the earth (Augustine) or whether it is being fulfilled by the saints in heaven (Kliefoth). It may be summed up in the idea that there will be no more millennium than there is now, and that the eternal state immediately follows the second coming of Christ. As they freely recognize that their concept of the millennium is quite foreign to the premillennial view they have been given the title

1

*amillennial* by most writers" (John F. Walvoord, *The Millennial Kingdom*, p. 6).

As Walvoord correctly states, amillenarians are opposed to the type of millennium taught by the premillennialist. They do not deny that Christ will reign over his saints on the earth. Rather, as Walvoord points out, they deny a *literal* (materialistic) reign. They also place this reign, as correctly pointed out by Walvoord, in a different point of time than does the premillenarian. They are also opposed to the type of millennium taught by the postmillennialist. They also place it at a different time in history than does the postmillenarian.

The term *amillennial* is a good descriptive term when used to describe an attitude toward the millennium put forth by the premillenarian or by the postmillenarian. For amillenarians admittedly do not believe in any such millennium. It is a misunderstood and unfortunate term, however, when applied to the teachings of the twentieth chapter of Revelation. For amillenarians do definitely believe in a biblical millennium.

Secondly, covenant theology is not a basic doctrine of amillennialism. An amillenarian may or may not hold to covenant theology. Many amillenarians do indeed hold to this theology, as do many postmillenarians and many premillenarians. The present writer disagrees with many of the presuppositions of covenant theology. And this would be true of a great many amillenarians known to this writer. Covenant theology, then, is not to be associated per se with amillennialism. The two doctrines do not stand or fall together.

Thirdly, there is no connection between Protestant amillennialism and Roman Catholicism. It is true that most Roman Catholic theologians are amillenarians. But it is also true that most Roman Catholic theologians believe in the virgin birth of Christ and many other sound doctrines. We are happy to say that most premillenarians also believe in the virgin birth. Yet it would be unfair, and unethical, and untrue, to accuse premillenarians of being bedfellows with Roman Catholics simply because they hold this and many other doctrines in common with Catholics. It is equally unfair, unethical, and untrue, to so brand amillenarians because they hold to amillennialism in common with Rome.

2

Fourthly, amillennialism is not liberalism. Amillenarians stand for a scriptural approach to eschatology. Their teachings are based squarely on the Bible as the inspired and infallible Word of God. It goes without saying that some liberal theologians hold the amillennial view of eschatology. But so do many liberals hold the other millennial views. Some of the most saintly Christians of all time have been amillenarians. And many outstanding conservative scholars today hold this view of the millennium. This fact will become obvious when we list some of the leading amillenarians.

Why has space been devoted here to a defense of amillennialism? Why has it seemed necessary to deny that amillenarians are tainted by either a negative view of the millennium as it is taught in the Bible, or Roman Catholicism, or liberalism; or that it holds, as a group, to covenant theology? The answer is simple. Critics have deliberately attempted to discredit amillenarians by charging them with these things. Some of these critics make outright accusations while others slander by association. Too often a misguided conception of amillennialism has kept sincere Christians from examining this school of thought *which has been the historic teaching of the church* since the days of Augustine or before. This was also the belief held by the great majority, if not indeed by all, of the Protestant reformers. It is the sincere hope of the writer that these preliminary refutations will pave the way for a positive and openminded examination of amillennialism.

What do amillenarians believe? Negatively speaking, they believe there will be no millennium as it is commonly described by premillenarians and postmillenarians. In this sense they are nonmillennial and gladly accept the title assigned to them. However, this is the only sense in which amillennialism can rightly be classed as a negative teaching. They have very positive beliefs about every doctrine plainly taught in the Scriptures — including a biblical millennium.

Although beliefs vary among amillenarians as to the exact time or place of the millennium, all are agreed that the New Testament places it before the second advent. Comparatively few amillenarians confine the millennium to a certain period within history. Augustine, for example, thought it would end in A.D. 650. Others might say it began at Pentecost and ended with the fall of

Rome in A.D. 476. These, however, as already indicated, make up a very small minority of those who hold to amillennialism. For the most part amillenarians could be divided into two main schools. One group would teach that the millennium refers to the intermediate state and is therefore enjoyed only by departed saints. Kliefoth brought forth this view about 1874. The other group, which would seem to be the larger group, believes the millennium began with the first advent of Chirst and will end with his second coming. This latter group believes all saints, living and dead, reign with Christ in the on-going millennium.

Amillenarians look on the Bible as a unit which contains no contradictions. They therefore believe that the book of Revelation says, symbolically, what the rest of the New Testament says in clear language. And the twentieth chapter of this symbolic book can be no exception. The one thousand year period is mentioned only in that chapter. Amillenarians take Revelation 20:1-6 as a symbolic picture of the interadvent period. They believe the expression "a thousand years" denotes a complete period of time, the length of which is known only by God. They believe that, in this twentieth chapter, John recapitulates what he has already covered, rather than dealing with a completely new period of time. In the entire book of Revelation John records seven visions dealing with the entire inter-advent period and closes out, in chapters 21 and 22, with the eternal state. This is why amillenarians find no scriptural basis for an interregnum between the second advent and the eternal state.

We believe entrance to the on-going millennium is gained solely through the new birth, and that John refers to this as the first resurrection. This is based on the many other places in the New Testament where the new birth is referred to specifically as a resur-rection. Such scriptures as Ephesians 2:1,5,6 and Colossians 2:13; 3:1 equate the new birth with a resurrection. And it is difficult for the amillenarian to conceive of more than one *first* resurrection just as it is difficult for him to accept more than one *last* trump. A complete section will be devoted later in this book to the scriptural teaching of the new birth as the Christian's first resurrection. Suffice it here to say that amillenarians believe that every person who is genuinely born again immediately becomes a child of the King and immediately begins an eternal reign with that King, and that the

4

present phase of that reign is a mere foretaste of what lies beyond the second coming and the ushering in of the eternal state.

Satan has only such power as God permits him to retain; this has always been the case. Christ came into the world, met Satan on his own ground, and, in fulfillment of Genesis 3:15, defeated Satan. This amillennialists firmly believe. They also believe that Revelation 20:1-3 speaks of this event. This too will be dealt with more fully later. Let it be said in passing that amillenarians find no contradiction whatsoever between two separate teachings found in the New Testament: (1) that Satan was bound with respect to one phase of his power (which is all that John says, with reference to binding, in Revelation) when Jesus died on the cross, and (2) that Satan still goes about as a roaring lion tempting, defying, deceiving, until Christ shall put him down finally with the brightness of his second coming.

Is the world getting better or worse? Postmillenarians say it is getting better, and that the preaching of the gospel will eventually see most of the world converted, thus ushering in an earthly millennium before the second coming. Premillenarians believe the world is growing increasingly worse, and that it will be at its very worst when Jesus returns. Amillenarians agree with the premillenarians on this point. Although we believe the kingdom of God began as a small mustard seed and grows steadily larger, we also believe that evil grows proportionately faster. Good and evil will exist side by side until the very harvest, which Jesus said will be the end of the world (Matt. 13:39). We believe this growth will culminate with the appearance of the antichrist, which Paul called the man of sin, and which John referred to as Satan being loosed for a little season. This loosing will take place in the very endtime of the present historical church age.

When it looks as though the man of sin actually will overcome God's followers, Christ will come on the scene and the devil will be cast eternally into the lake of fire. At this second coming of Christ — which will be a literal, visible, bodily coming — a number of scriptures will be fulfilled almost simultaneously. All the graves will be opened; all saints living at that time, along with all who have died in the Lord, will be given new spiritual bodies; all saints will be raptured together to meet the Lord in the air for the purpose of

5

escorting their King to the earth; this general resurrection then will be followed by a general judgment, in which the saints will take part because of their standing in Christ; the earth will be cleansed of all sin; and the eternal state will be ushered in. At the sound of the trumpet which signals the second coming of Christ, all destinies are eternally sealed, the day of salvation closes, and every person who has rejected Christ until that point in time (be he Jew or Gentile) will spend eternity in hell while every believer of every generation will enjoy eternity as a member of the one body of Christ.

This is a very brief outline of amillennial beliefs. These beliefs will be dealt with in more detail in subsequent chapters. May the Lord enlighten our understanding of the faith once delivered to the saints.

## II

## A HISTORY OF AMILLENNIALISM

The name is new, and there have been times in history when these teachings were not pronounced with vigor. But amillennial teachings are as old as Christianity itself. Amillennialism has always been the majority view of the historic Christian church, even as it remains today. What has come to be known as amillennialism was held by the great majority of the church fathers, the Protestant reformers, and the most reputable Bible commentaries.

Dr. John F. Walvoord, himself a dispensational premillennialist and editor of the magazine *Bibliotheca Sacra*, admits that "Reformed eschatology has been predominantly amillennial. Most if not all of the leaders of the Protestant Reformation were amillennial in their eschatology, following the teachings of Augustine" (issue of Jan.-March, 1951).

Speaking of amillennialism, Dr. Louis Berkhof says: "Some premillennialists have spoken of Amillennialism as a new view and as one of the most recent novelties, but this is certainly not in accord with the testimony of history. The name is indeed new, but the view to which it is applied is as old as Christianity. It had at least as many advocates as Chiliasm among the Church Fathers of the second and third centuries, supposed to have been the heyday of Chiliasm. It has ever since been the view most widely accepted, is the only view that is either expressed or implied in the great historical Confessions of the Church, and has always been the prevalent view in Reformed circles" (*Systematic Theology*, p. 708).

Dr. Loraine Boettner, who holds to the postmillennial view, says: "At the present time Amillennialism is the official view of the conservative Missouri Synod Lutheran Church, which has a membership of more than 2,000,000 and sponsors a world-wide 'Lutheran Hour' radio program. It is also the view of the equally conservative Christian Reformed Church, likewise sponsoring an extensive radio

7

program known as the 'Back to God Hour,' and two of the smaller Presbyterian bodies, The Orthodox Presbyterian Church, and the Reformed Presbyterian Church. It is ably set forth in two of the most conservative and scholarly theological seminaries in the United States, Calvin Seminary, in Grand Rapids, Michigan, and Westminster Theological Seminary, in Philadelphia, Pennsylvania" (*The Millennium*, p. 112).

One could build upon the words of Dr. Boettner and say that amillennialism is the belief held by a great majority of all denominational seminaries in the United States. Unfortunately, most of these schools are not as vocal on eschatology as are those seminaries mentioned by Boettner; but if they were pinned down this would prove to be the majority belief among their professors. On the other hand, dispensational premillennialism is being taught by just about every undenominational Bible school in this country. The exceptions would merely prove the rule if a survey were taken among schools.

The following comment seems apropos here: "Many, perhaps most, Calvinists, not to mention evangelicals other than Reformed, do not share Warfield's post-millennialism. Both of his great Calvinistic contemporaries, Kuyper and Bavinck, for instance, were a-millennialists, as was his esteemed colleague, Geerhardus Vos, perhaps the most erudite advocate of a-millennialism in America. He himself freely admitted that a-millennialism, though not known in those days under that name, is the historic Protestant view, as expressed in the creeds of the Reformation period including the Westminster Standards" (p. xxxix, *Biblical and Theological Studies*, Benjamin B. Warfield; this statement is from the biographical chapter written by the editor, Samuel G. Craig).

Augustine (A.D. 400) usually is credited with having crystallized amillennial teachings, while at the same time sounding the death knell to chiliasm. One could almost name endlessly those who have swelled the ranks of this school of thought. Included in a listing would be Martin Luther, Melancthon, Zwingli, Knox, John Calvin, William Hendriksen, William Masselink, William J. Grier, Louis Berkhof, Martin Wyngaarden, George L. Murray, Floyd Hamilton, Albertus Pieters, Geerhardus Vos, Abraham Kuyper, William Rutgers, Edward McDowell, Ray Summers, Herschel Hobbs, and many, many others.

8

Now that a portion of the amillennial family tree has been given, let me hasten to say that we do not rest our case on the fact that these beliefs have been held by any man or group of men. The all-important question is "What saith the scripture?" While it is good and comforting to know that great conservative students of the Bible have held like beliefs as ours, this does not make it true to the Word of God. Paul said we were to let God be true even if it makes every man a liar (Rom. 3:4).

Altogether too much energy has been spent in trying to prove which church father held which millennial theory. Strangely enough most of this tracing, and claiming, is done by dispensationalists. And while some of the men they list were premillennialists, they were by no stretch of the imagination dispensationalists. Indeed, modern dispensationalism did not even come into existence until the nineteenth century. Some dispensational writers have been dishonest at this point. For they have claimed that Augustine was a dispensationalist in their sense of the word. They quote an isolated statement made by Augustine wherein he spoke of properly dividing the dispensations as one studied the Bible. These writers fail to point out, however, that Augustine did not give the word *dispensation* the same connotation placed on it by modern dispensationalists. Nor do they point out that the only divisions (dispensations) Augustine had in mind were two — the period covered in the Old Testament as over against the period of time covered by the New Testament.

Several other observations need to be made with reference to the way in which dispensational premillennialists attempt to trace their beliefs back to the early centuries A.D. They make blanket claims about men whose millennial beliefs are not known with any degree of certainty. They imply that their beliefs (*dispensational* premillennialism) were held by the early church fathers, when, actually, there is very little similarity between historic premillennialism and modern dispensationalism. Most of the men whom dispensationalists claim as doctrinal ancestors had never heard of the basic teachings of modern dispensationalism. The reason for this is simple: these beliefs had not been born! Most chiliasts of the early centuries after Christ had no teachings about a secret rapture, a distinction between Israel and the church, postponement theories, or many other innovations of dispensationalism. About the only thing these groups had in common is the belief that a millennium will be set up on the earth after the second coming of Christ.

When we practice or teach a thing we should be able to give New Testament authority for so doing. One has a rather weak position whenever he has to resort to quoting the writings of men — even though these writings may be the Didache, Apostles' Creed, or some other church creed. There is a vast difference between the writings of uninspired men and those of inspired Bible writers. And the proximity of an extra-canonical writer to the first century does not make his writings any more authoritative. We should keep in mind that heresy began even before the death of the apostles, and that it ran rampant immediately after the death of the last apostle. So that heresy — whether it originated in the first or the twentieth century — is still heresy.

Indeed, even when we quote the New Testament we must be careful that we are quoting something sanctioned therein and not some wrong practice which is merely *recorded* therein. Let me illustrate the point. The New Testament records the fact that a professing Christian took his father's wife to be his own wife. Could one build a doctrine upon this? It's in the Bible. But does this practice have a biblical basis? The answer is obvious. Or take the case of those who made drunken feasts of the Lord's Supper. Would we build upon this? The Bible records many evil practices, yet it nowhere condones evil.

Jesus told his disciples that they were not yet ready to comprehend many of his teachings, but that after his ascension the Holy Spirit would enlighten them. The New Testament records the fact that after the resurrection the disciples remembered some of the teachings of Jesus, and that they then — for the first time — understood his teachings on certain matters. This explains why the disciples asked our Lord some foolish questions before his death. Their minds were still filled with Judaism, and their questions came from the Talmud rather than from the Bible. In most cases, it would seem, our Lord did not bother to rebuke them for their incorrect questions. If he answered at all, however, he always gave them a scriptural answer. He left much of their education to the future work of the Holy Spirit. Peter's housetop experience (Acts 10:9-16) was a part of his continuing education as God patiently cleared

Peter's mind of rules which were not to be carried out under the new covenant.

Every Christian who accepts the Bible as the divinely inspired, infallible Word of God will accept *every* teaching of the Bible as authoritative. This cannot be said, however, of any other writing regardless of its date. It is dangerous to equate any man's teachings with those of the Scriptures — be the man Luther, Calvin, Scofield, or anyone else. Many persons use names such as these as a final authority for theological teachings. I should have said they are used to prove *certain* theological teachings. For the thinking person has never lived who would not hasten to divorce himself from some of the teachings and practices of these men. Yet, they rest securely on these men for authority for individual doctrines.

So where should we trace our doctrine? To the New Testament, and only there. And even this statement must be qualified. We should trace our doctrine to that which the New Testament lays down as a teaching or practice. These teachings should be distinguished from the incorrect practices which the New Testament records, but condemns. We need to keep in mind that much of the New Testament was written to correct unscriptural teachings and practices of individuals and churches.

Even the statements of the apostles should be labeled "before Calvary," and "after Calvary." Before Calvary, while they were learners (disciples) at the feet of Jesus, their minds still retained many Jewish fables. One example must suffice here. Their indoctrination from the Talmud and from the Jewish religious leaders had fixed in their minds the idea that the Jewish temple would stand as long as the world stood. Therefore when Jesus stated that the temple would be destroyed, they immediately jumped to the wrong conclusion that he spoke of the end of the world, when actually he spoke of the destruction of Jerusalem by the Roman armies in A.D. 70.

"And Jesus went out from the temple, and was going on his way; and his disciples came to him to show him the buildings of the temple. But he answered and said unto them, See ye not all these things? Verily I say unto you, There shall not be left here one stone upon another, that shall not be thrown down" (Matt. 24:1, 2). This is the statement of Jesus which prompted a Jewish question from his Jewish disciples. Note that the statement is simply to the effect that the temple will be utterly destroyed.

Now let us examine the question which this statement caused to be formed in the minds of the disciples. "And as he sat on the mount of Olives, the disciples came unto him privately, saying, Tell us, when shall these things be? and what shall be the sign of thy coming, and of the end of the world?" (Matt. 24:3).

Matthew records, in this setting, one statement by Jesus: that the temple would be destroyed. And he records one question by the disciples, which was prompted by the one statement. Yes, it was one question, although a three-part question. In the disciples' minds they were asking about three things that would happen simultaneously — the destruction of the temple, the second coming of Christ, and the end of the world. Their Jewish minds could not conceive of the world continuing to stand longer than the temple stood. History, however, has proved them wrong.

We have been discussing the "before Calvary" disciples. These men were still learners in the Messiah's seminary. Before they would be ready to serve as God's amanuenses to write the New Testament they must complete this schooling plus a postgraduate course to be taught by the Holy Spirit. It was the "after Calvary" disciples who wrote the New Testament.

Much that is put forth today as being New Testament doctrine is actually nothing more than the Jewish fables which were recorded in the New Testament, but which also were soundly rebuked by Jesus and later by his disciples. These are the teachings rejected by amillenarians today. They do not reject the teachings of the New Testament, but they do decisively reject the rabbinic teachings of the Pharisees. They reject the materialistic kingdom (millennium) demanded by the Pharisees, but they accept and proclaim the spiritual kingdom (millennium) outlined by our Lord.

Amillenarians are happy in the fact that many great conservative students of the Bible have been of like belief with them. However, amillennial beliefs are not based on any men or man-made creeds. They rest their convictions solely on a clear searching of the infallible Word of God. In our next chapter we shall see how amillenarians interpret the Bible.

# III

## HERMENEUTICS

One very basic conflict between different millennial groups is their hermeneutics — the manner in which they interpret the Bible. In fact, this difference is what divides equally conservative men into differing camps with reference to the millennium. This fact is acknowledged frequently by all millennial schools of thought. Each of the millennial views has been held by conservative, scholarly men who were devoted to a correct interpretation of the Bible. And all have looked on the Scriptures as divinely inspired, and as the Christian's only rule of faith and life.

No one millennial school has ever had a corner on conservative Christian scholars. Each of the three main schools — historic premillennialism, postmillennialism, and amillennialism — has a roll call of notable conservative giants of the faith. The different millennial views have arisen, not because of indifference toward the Bible, but simply because men interpreted the Word of God in a different manner. A few quotations will bear out this statement.

These statements are from the pen of a dispensationalist. "There is a growing realization in the theological world that the crux of the millennial issue is the question of the *method* of interpreting Scripture. Premillenarians follow the so-called 'grammatical-historical' literal interpretation while amillenarians use a spiritualizing method" (John Walvoord, *The Millennial Kingdom*, p. 50). "A proper study of the millennial issue demands, first, an analysis of the methods of interpretation which have produced amillennialism and premillennialism. This lays bare the problem and opens the way to see the issue in its true light" (*Ibid.*, p. 62).

Now a word, to this same effect, by an amillenarian. "The issue, then, between amillennialism and premillennialism is their respective methods of interpretation, and little progress can be made in the study of the millennial issue until this aspect is analyzed and under-

13

stood" (Albertus Pieters, *The Leader,* September 5, 1934, as cited by Gerrit H. Hospers, *The Principle of Spiritualization in Hermeneutics,* p. 5).

The above quotations make clear the fact that all students of the millennium point to one basic conflict between the various schools. That conflict is the manner in which each school of thought interprets the Scriptures. Since this book is essentially an examination of amillennialism, just how does the amillenarian interpret Scripture? In giving the answer to this question we are confronted with a paradox: *conservative amillenarians interpret the Bible in exactly the same manner claimed to be used by conservative millenarians in each of the other schools!* All conservative groups, including the futurist and the dispensationalist, claim to use the grammatical-historical literal method of interpreting Scripture. Let us look at some examples of this fact.

We have already quoted Dr. Walvoord to the effect that his school of thought used the grammatical-historical literal method of interpretation. Here is a quote from Dr. Pieters pointing out that amillenarians use this exact same method of interpretation. "No one defends or employs the allegorizing method of exegesis. Calvin and the other great Bible students of the Reformation saw clearly that the method was wrong and taught the now generally accepted 'grammatical-historical' literal interpretation, so far as the Scriptures in general are concerned. That they retain the spiritualizing method in expounding many of the prophecies was because they found themselves forced to do so in order to be faithful to the New Testament" (Albertus Pieters, *Darbyism Vs. The Historical Faith*, Calvin Forum, II, 225-28, May, 1936).

We see then that all conservative students of the Bible use the grammatical-historical literal approach to the Scriptures. But these groups all have one other practice in common: each millennial group — while it interprets *most* of the Bible in this literal manner — also interprets *parts* of the Bible in a spiritual or figurative manner. Now there would be nothing unusual about this fact, except for one amazing thing: premillenarians — especially dispensational premillenarians — freely use the method while maligning other groups for doing the same thing that they themselves do!

As a matter of fact, blanket statements made by ardent premillenarians lead many unwary readers to believe that (1) all

Scripture is spiritualized by the amillenarian, while (2) all Scripture is interpreted literally by premillenarians. The statement by Walvoord, which we quoted earlier, is an example of this technique: "Premillenarians follow the so-called 'grammatical-historical' literal interpretation while amillenarians use a spiritualizing method" (*The Millennial Kingdom*, p. 59). Many such blanket statements are to be found throughout the writings of men such as Walvoord. And only as one reads other conflicting statements by these same writers does he realize that this is not the whole truth. Nor is it *wholly* the truth.

On page 62 of this same book Dr. Walvoord admits that amillenarians actually do not apply the spiritual method to all the Bible. "The amillennial method of interpreting Scripture is correctly defined as the spiritualizing method. It is clear, however, that conservative amillennialists limit the use of this method, and in fact adopt the literal method of interpreting most of the Scripture." Two things ought to be pointed out with regard to this statement by Dr. Walvoord. (1) It definitely contradicts his blanket statement of page 59, and (2) there are two conflicting statements within this last quote from page 62 of his book: for he begins the paragraph by saying that the amillennial method of interpreting Scripture is the spiritualizing method; then he ends the same paragraph by saying that conservative amillennialists interpret *most of the Scripture* in a literal manner. Which statement does he really mean to stand by?

Let us look at another contradictory statement on this subject. This quotation is from page 71 of *The Millennial Kingdom*: "While amillenarians reject the figurative method of interpreting the Bible as a general method, it is used extensively not only in the interpretation of prophecy but in other areas of theology as well." This is a relatively true statement. However, it contradicts his blanket statements elsewhere that the spiritualizing method is *the* method of interpretation used by amillenarians.

One more statement from Dr. Walvoord must suffice on this particular point. "Amillenarians use two methods of interpretation, the spiritualizing method for prophecy and the literal method for other Scriptures" (p. 63, *The Millennial Kingdom*). Here is yet a different blanket statement which contradicts statements made elsewhere in Walvoord's book as to how amillennialists interpret the Bible. Here he says they spiritualize [all] prophecy while they

15

interpret [all] the rest of Scripture literally. We quoted him before as saying amillenarians used the spiritualizing method *extensively* in all parts of the Bible. Here he says this is restricted to their interpretation of prophecy alone.

What Dr. Walvoord should have said is that amillenarians use a spiritual interpretation on *some* scriptures, including *some* of the prophecies. This would have been a true statement. However, this would be nothing more than could be said of premillenarians, including Dr. Walvoord's dispensationalist school of thought.

These contradictory and inflammatory statements by Walvoord lead us to one of two conclusions: either his blind spot keeps him from seeing the true method of interpretation used by amillenarians, or he deliberately sets out to poison his readers' minds by using half-truths.

And what about Dr. Walvoord's group? Do they — as his blanket statements indicate — interpret Scripture by a totally different method from that used by amillenarians? Let Dr. Walvoord answer this question for us. "Most premillenarians would agree with Hamilton that obvious figurative language or instances where the New Testament gives authority for interpreting the Old Testament in other than a literal sense would be just grounds for use of the spiritualizing method. Obviously, some Scriptures of the Old Testament and a few passages of the New Testament have a figurative meaning" (*The Millennial Kingdom*, p. 65).

It is difficult to believe that the above statement was made by the same man, who preaches in that same book that premillenarians are the only "good guys" because they use the grammatical-historical literal method of interpreting Scripture, and that amillenarians are defiant "bad guys" because they spiritualize parts of the Bible. For here he admits that premillenarians do exactly what he criticizes amillenarians for doing, i.e., they recognize figurative language in parts of the Bible. One can only wonder what it is that makes one group out to be liberals on the specific grounds that they spiritualize parts of Scripture, while another group does the same thing and parades as stalwart defenders of the faith.

Another case wherein the pot calls the kettle black is Walvoord's accusation that amillenarians lack objectivity in their approach to the Scriptures. "It was shown that the only rule which could be followed by the amillenarian was hopelessly subjective — the figurative method was used whenever the amillenarian found it necessary to change the literal meaning of Scripture to conform to his ideas" (*The Millennial Kingdom,* p. 71).

Just how objective are the premillenarians in their interpretation of Scripture? One example should suffice here. In order to get this example clearly before us we first quote a verse of Scripture: "After this *I* looked, and, behold, a door was opened in heaven: and the first voice which I heard was as it were of a trumpet talking with *me*; which said, Come up hither, and I will shew *thee* things which must be hereafter" (Rev. 4:1, italics added). What does this verse say? Well, it says to *John* that *John* will be taken up higher and that *John* will be shown things which must happen after the time the voice was speaking. Ah, but is this what it says? Let us see now the objectivity with which the dispensational premillenarian approaches this verse. He says — and bases much of his entire teaching on this — that the voice actually was saying to the *church* that the *church* should come up higher and that the *church* would be shown things to come. And when will this verse be fulfilled? Well, the amillenarian would say that it happened — to John — nearly two thousand years ago. But not so, says Dr. Walvoord's group. They say it will not be fulfilled until the church is raptured.

And what is their reason for so interpreting Revelation 4:1? The answer is simple: these people teach that the church will not go through the tribulation; and since the book of Revelation takes some group of God's people through much tribulation, a problem exists which threatens the very premise of the dispensational argument. Solution? Remove the church from the book of Revelation. But it cannot be removed from the first three chapters since the church is there called by name. So? Remove it from the remainder of the book. And how do they apply the grammatical-historical literal method of interpretation? The answer is simple. John was inspired to write that the voice spoke to him; however, it actually was speaking to the church; therefore, there is no mention of the church — or reference to it — from 4:1 on to the end of the book. Therefore it is obvious, say the premillenarians, that Revelation 4 through 19 deals only with national Israel and that everything recorded in chapters 4 through 19 will take place during a seven-year period following the rapture of the Christian church. And where did this seven-year period come from? Why it was postponed after sixty-nine of Daniel's seventy weeks were fulfilled by the first advent. And how does one arrive at all these presuppositions? Simple, says Dr. Walvoord; merely use the grammatical-historical literal method of interpreting Scripture. And, by all means, be objective!

What we have just outlined is a dispensationalist interpretation of a verse of Scripture. This is not the interpretation of the amillenarian, who, according to Walvoord, is "hopelessly subjective," and who uses the figurative method whenever he finds it necessary "to change the literal meaning of Scripture to conform to his ideas." Yes, Walvoord is very critical of the amillenarians for what he calls their "strained exegesis."

Since all conservative men use essentially the same method of interpreting Scripture, then how is it that they end up with such divergent views on the millennium? Does the Bible, when approached from the grammatical-historical literal point of view, actually give five completely different accounts of the millennium? No, the different teachings come about because of inconsistency of interpretation—because of the inconsistent use of the known rules of hermeneutics. To be more specific, our differences head up in one major problem. That problem is the hyperliteral interpretation of certain — and only certain — verses of Scripture in order to justify preconceived unscriptural presuppositions. Although no human is free from this error, an overuse of the practice brought about the alleged earthly materialistic millennium of the millenarians — pre- and postmillennial. A secondary problem is the act of taking verses out of their context; however, the paramount problem lies in basing presuppositions on a hyperliteral interpretation of certain passages of the Bible.

Let us illustrate this point. We find a case of hyperliteralism in the writings of Loraine Boettner — an outstanding spokesman for post-millenarians. Dr. Boettner argues for a literal fulfillment of certain Old Testament passages: "What shall we say, for instance, to the following? Isaiah 2:2-4: 'And it shall come to pass in the latter days, that the mountain of Jehovah's house shall be established on the top of the mountains, and shall be exalted above the hills; and all nations shall flow unto it. And many nations shall go and say, Come ye, and let us go up to the mountain of Jehovah, to the house of the God of Jacob; and he will teach us of his ways, and we will walk in his paths; for out of Zion shall go forth the law, and the word of Jehovah from Jerusalem. And he will judge between the nations, and will decide concerning many prophets; and they shall beat their swords into plowshares, and their spears into pruning hooks; nation shall not lift up sword against nation, neither shall they learn war anymore' " (*The Millennium,* p. 119).

Dr. Boettner asks what shall we say about this passage. Well, we would say about it the same thing we would say about similar passages. For example, we know of no known millennialists who insist on a literal fulfillment of the passage with reference to John the Baptist making the hills and valleys level one with the other. This, and myriads of other such passages, are accepted as being in symbolical language. Passages such as Isaiah 2:2-4 have two possible fulfillments. One possible fulfillment is to be found in the present day, i.e., such as all ground being level at the foot of the cross, or as a lion (such as Paul before his conversion) lying down with a lamb (such as Barnabas). Another possible fulfillment lies in the eternal state. Only here will the utopia of swords being beaten into plowshares truly be realized.

It ought to be pointed out that refusal to place a literal interpretation upon a given passage of the Bible does not make that passage any less meaningful and true. Dr. Boettner remarks (p. 119) that the amillennial position leaves a continent of prophecies unexplained. He goes on to state that many passages "surely foretell a future golden age *of some kind"* (italics added). Now here is the real crux of the argument between millenarians and amillenarians; amillenarians too believe in a golden age "of some kind." Our differences are not as to whether a golden age was prophesied, but rather the kind of golden age the prophets had in mind. The millenarians say it was to be a materialistic earthly golden age. Amillenarians say, on the other hand, that the golden age will not be fully realized until the eternal state arrives. Rather than being limited to a duration of one thousand years, this golden age will last throughout eternity.

Indeed, Dr. Boettner answers his own argument with reference to Isaiah 2:2-4. For on page 120 he makes a statement most of which would pass for amillennial teaching. Having stated that Micah 4:1-5 is a restatement of Isaiah 2:2-4, Dr. Boettner says: "Here, *in figurative language and under Old Testament terminology of*

*Mount Zion and the house of Jehovah, — which was the only termi-*
*nology that the people to whom this prophecy was given would have*
*been able to understand —* was predicted the world-wide conquest
and dominion of the Church, A Christianized people, dwelling
securely, free from the devastations of war, and doing righteously.
*In other places of Scripture the mountain of Jehovah's house is*
*spiritualized to mean the Church. See particularly Hebrews 12:22,*
*where, speaking of the Church it is said: 'But ye are come unto*
*mount Zion, and unto the city of the living God, the heavenly*
*Jerusalem. . . .' In Isaiah 2 we are taught that the Church is to be*
*prominent, like a house on the top of the mountain, or like a*
*mountain on a plain,* and that its guidance will be sought willingly
in all phases of human life — in the spiritual, social, economic and
political realms. The statement that 'all peoples shall flow unto it'
must mean that people all over the world are to be Christians, and
that they will seek to know God's will as it is made known to them
through his Word. *Their beating their swords into plowshares, and*
*their spears into pruning hooks, is clearly figurative language, a figure*
*appropriate for the time in which this prophecy was given,* but to be
fulfilled in a far distant age in which the nations would not spend
their energies and substance in destructive wars, — 'Nation shall not
lift up sword against nation, neither shall they learn war any more.'
*To 'sit every man under his vine and under his fig tree' is again a*
*figure appropriate to that day and age,* a symbol of contented
peaceful home life, pointing forward to a time of world-wide righteousness on which alone true peace can be based" (*The Millennium,*
p. 120, italics added).

Here again one can see that the millenarian wants to be
hyperliteral only in dealing with certain choice passages. This fact is
evident as Dr. Boettner continues: "Isaiah 11:1-10: 'And there
shall come forth a shoot out of the stock of Jesse, and a branch out
of his roots shall bear fruit. And the Spirit of Jehovah shall rest
upon him, the spirit of wisdom and understanding, the spirit of
counsel and might, the spirit of knowledge and of the fear of
Jehovah. And his delight shall be in the fear of Jehovah; and he shall
not judge after the sight of his eyes, neither decide after the
hearing of his ears; but with righteousness shall he judge the poor,
and decide with equity for the meek of the earth; and he shall smite
the earth with the rod of his mouth; and with the breath of his lips

20

shall he slay the wicked. And righteousness shall be the girdle of his waist, and faithfulness the girdle of his loins. . . .

"And it shall come to pass in that day, that the root of Jesse, that standeth for an ensign of the peoples, unto him shall the nations seek; and his resting place shall be glorious' " (*Ibid.,* pp. 120-21).

Here one might wax hyperliteral and throw Dr. Boettner's words back at him — "What shall we say about passages such as these?" In other words, when did a literal shoot come forth out of the stock of Jesse? Or a branch out of his roots? Or when did Christ ever literally smite the earth with a rod? Dr. Boettner no doubt would hasten to answer that these were figurative prophecies fulfilled in the Christ. And the amillenarian would readily agree. The amillenarian, however, would go further to say that the alleged millennial passages fall into this same obvious category.

Dr. Boettner states that Isaiah 11:9 loses its force when taken in any other than a postmillennial sense. "Similarly, swords and plowshares, and spears and pruning hooks, spoken of in Isaiah 2:4, cannot be thought of as having any place in heaven. This is, of course, figurative language. It foretells an age of peace, contentment and safety right here on this earth." In reply to this, one merely needs to ask whether streets, or trees, or medicine, or rivers have any place in heaven. For the Bible (see for example Revelation 22) says that all of these will be present in heaven.

To continue our examples of hyperliteralism we quote now from the pen of a dispensational premillenarian. "The viewpoint of Old Testament prophecies is that the saints on earth at the time of the second advent will enter the millennial kingdom in the flesh, an obvious contradiction of the idea of translation. This is clearly taught by the fact that saints will till the ground, raise crops, and have children born to them, all of which would be quite incredible for translation saints" (*The Millennial Kingdom,* Walvoord, p. 242).

Here Dr. Walvoord practices the art of circular reasoning. First he presupposes an earthly future millennium. Then he further presupposes that the saints will enter this alleged kingdom in human form without undergoing translation of their bodies. He builds on these two presuppositions — without offering scriptural proof of either — a hyperliteral interpretation of biblical passages referring to rewards of God's people. He concludes by stating that these

21

(hyperliteral) earthly pursuits would never be carried out by translated saints.

Here again one need merely ask one question of Dr. Walvoord: The saints of the New Jerusalem in Revelation 22 who will be surrounded by fruits, medicinal leaves, gates, rivers, streets — will they be translated saints? Or will they still be in human bodies?

We have said that millenarians apply hyperliteral interpretations to only certain selected passages of Scripture. Let us prove this point. A. C. Gaebelein is another prominent spokesman for dispensational premillenarians. In dealing with Daniel 12:2, Dr. Gaebelein has this to say: "The physical resurrection is not taught in the second verse of this chapter, if it were the passage would be in clash with the revelation concerning resurrection in the New Testament. There is no general resurrection. . . . We repeat the passage has nothing to do with physical resurrection. Physical resurrection is however used as a figure of the national revival of Israel in that day. They have been sleeping nationally in the dust of the earth, buried among the Gentiles. But at that time there will take place a national restoration, a bringing together of the house of Judah and the house of Israel" (A. C. Gaebelein, *The Prophet Daniel*, p. 200).

It is difficult to believe that the above statement came from the pen of one who insists on a hyperliteral interpretation of other passages from the same Bible which contains these plain words. It has been the historical church teaching since apostolic times that Daniel 12:2 speaks of the physical resurrection. This, however, does not tie in with a favorite "rediscovered truth" of this hyperliteral teacher. Therefore, he makes a new and arbitrary rule for himself and says this one passage deviates from his rule of literalism. Here; he says, the *bodies* and *dust* and *graves* spoken of by Daniel really refer to a captivity and return of national Israel! Oh consistency, where art thou?

We stated earlier that each of us is liable to fall into the snare of hyperliteralism. It would seem that some amillenarians have succumbed on occasions. We refer to those who insist that Revelation 20:4 refers to disembodied souls, thereby confining the millennial reign to heaven or the intermediate state. The Bible speaks, in numerous places, of living people as souls. For example, in the book of Genesis we read that eight *souls* entered the ark. These were living embodied souls of people who were very earthly and

22

still very much alive. The interested reader will find many other such scriptural examples.

It is indeed a dangerous thing for *anyone* to wax hyperliteral — especially in dealing with highly figurative language found in some parts of the Bible.

Hyperliteralism is the same interpretation given to certain passages from the Old Testament by the Pharisees of Jesus' day. It was this method of interpretation that, humanly speaking, kept them from recognizing the Christ as the Hope of Israel. Hyperliteralism kept them from seeing that the unfulfilled promises of the Old Testament were to be fulfilled through the Christian church. Rabbinism is still with us today, in modern garb.

The non-believing Jews expected their Messiah to appear and to set up a kingdom. And this belief was based on the Scriptures. However, their hyperliteral interpretation of the Old Testament blinded their eyes to the genuine kingdom and kept them from recognizing the real king. The Messiah did come into the world, and he did establish his kingdom; or, rather he manifested a new phase of the on-going eternal kingdom of God.

The Jews expected a warrior-type Messiah who would inflict vengeance on their enemies and place Jews in chosen places of leadership. To their dismay Jesus did not come into Jerusalem on a white charger, but rather he entered the city on a lowly donkey. And he went about as a physician — healing even Gentiles! And he taught them to love their enemies and to do good to those who hated them. Away with such a "messiah"! This cannot be the Messiah of our Talmud. And deliver us from such a "kingdom" as this person offers; surely this is not the kingdom of our Talmud. Indeed, Mr. Pharisee, you are correct. Jesus was not the "messiah" of the Talmud. But he was, and is, the Messiah predicted in the language (oftentimes figurative language) of the Old Testament. And, while his kingdom was a disappointment to hyperliteral interpreters of the Old Testament, it was indeed the fulfillment of the kingdom predicted therein.

Even John the Baptist had his moment of doubt. He proclaimed what God inspired him to preach, yet he did not fully understand all these teachings. If this be the Messiah then why did he not establish an earthly kingdom? And why was John — the Messiah's forerunner — suffering imprisonment? Finally John's doubts grew until he could contain his perplexities no longer, so he sent some of his disciples to ask Jesus a very pointed question. "Now when John heard in the prison the works of the Christ, he sent by his disciples and said unto him, Art thou he that cometh, or look we for another?" (Matt. 11:2,3).

Jesus' answer to John was not a yes or no answer. He merely directed John to restudy the Old Testament picture of the Messiah and then to compare this picture with the actual works of Jesus. "And Jesus answered and said unto them, Go and tell John the things which ye hear and see: the blind receive their sight, and the lame walk, the lepers are cleansed, and the deaf hear, and the dead are raised up, and the poor have good tidings preached to them. And blessed is he, whosoever shall find no occasion of stumbling in me" (Matt. 11:4-6).

But what of John's understanding, from God himself, that Jesus came to bring judgment and separation? And where was the fan with which Messiah was to sweep clean the floor of his kingdom? Were these promises untrue? Or are they to be relegated entirely to the future? No. John himself taught that the first advent represented the ax of judgment being placed at the root of the tree of God's kingdom (Matt. 3:10-12). The winnowing — the separating of the wheat from the chaff — is already in motion, and will be consummated at the second coming.

To return now to our basic question in this chapter: how do amillenarians interpret the Bible? Floyd Hamilton makes a good representative statement on this point. He says: "But if we reject the literal method of interpretation as the universal rule for the interpretation of all prophecies, how are we to interpret them? Well, of course, there are many passages in prophecy that were meant to be taken literally. In fact a good working rule to follow is that the literal interpretation of the prophecy is to be accepted unless (a) the passages contain obviously figurative language, or (b) unless the New Testament gives authority for interpreting them in other than a literal sense, or (c) unless a literal interpretation would produce a contradiction with truths, principles, or factual statements contained in non-symbolic books of the New Testament. Another obvious rule to be followed is that the clearest New Testament passages in non-symbolic books are to be the norm for the interpretation of prophecy,

24

rather than obscure or partial revelations contained in the Old Testament. In other words we should accept the clear and plain parts of Scripture as a basis for getting the true meaning of the more difficult parts of Scripture" (*Basis of Millennial Faith,* pp. 53-54).

It is incorrect for anyone to say that amillenarians (as a group) take all prophecy in a spiritual sense, and all other Scripture literally. It is more nearly correct to say that we take all Scripture literally except where the context or related passages require that it be taken otherwise. It should also be reiterated that amillenarians take *all* passages as the inspired Word of God. We find stronger lessons, sometimes, in a figurative language than can be packed into a literal rendering of some passages. It is all the Word of God, and — whether written figuratively or literally — every passage has a spiritual message for God's people, while every passage is literally true.

# IV

## SALVATION

". . . The fact that all the saints of all dispensations are saved on the basis of the death of Christ is interpreted as a just ground for concluding that the term *church* is properly used of saints in both the Old and New Testaments. Hence Jews and Gentiles who were saved in the Old Testament period are considered as included in the New Testament church. *In fact, the usual tendency is to deny any essential difference in the nature of their salvation*" (John F. Walvoord, *The Millennial Kingdom*, pp. 80-81, italics added).

These words are from the pen of one who holds nothing but contempt for amillennialism. Yet he has described accurately the amillennial belief about salvation. Dr. Walvoord also correctly points out that soteriology (the study of salvation) represents one of the paramount differences between amillenarians and dispensational premillenarians.

What exactly do we mean by salvation? Salvation is a comprehensive term, embracing such doctrines as election, atonement, adoption, forgiveness, justification, reconciliation, regeneration, assurance, and glorification. All of these, and others, are involved in scriptural salvation. The English term is derived from the Latin *salvare*, meaning "to save," and from *salus*, which means "health," or "help." The Greek equivalent to salvation is *soteria*. (This is why theologians use the term soteriology in referring to salvation.) This Greek word can mean "cure," "recovery," "redemption," "remedy," "rescue," "welfare," "salvation." We see then that the *meaning* of salvation is much larger than the term itself.

In God's progressive revelation in the Bible salvation is used early in the Old Testament to refer to the physical deliverance of God's people from their enemies, from sickness, and from other physical dangers. As one progresses through the Scriptures, however, it becomes evident that salvation has also to do with *spiritual* deliverance. In the New Testament one arrives at the real primary meaning of this word — deliverance from sin. God, through Christ, *is* man's salvation; and man's greatest need for deliverance is redemption from the stranglehold of sin.

Salvation is embodied in Jesus Christ and his willing sacrifice on Calvary. "God was in Christ reconciling the world unto himself" (II Cor. 5:19). Simeon had the baby Jesus in his arms when he said "For mine eyes have seen *thy salvation,* which thou hast prepared before the face of all peoples; a light for revelation to the Gentiles, And the Glory of thy people Israel" (Luke 2:30). And Jesus apparently spoke of himself when he said to Zacchaeus, "Today is *salvation* come to this house" (Luke 19:9). No doubt his statement also referred to the deliverance of Zacchaeus resulting from Jesus' visit; however, the deliverance was by and through Jesus himself.

"But when the fulness of the time came, God sent forth his Son, born of a woman, born under the law, that he might redeem them that were under the law, that we might receive the adoption of sons. And because ye are sons, God sent forth the Spirit of his Son into our hearts, crying, Abba, Father" (Gal. 4:4-6).

The following story well illustrates how our Lord is the embodiment of salvation. A son had willfully disobeyed his father's rule. As punishment for the disobedience, the father told the son that he must spend three days in the attic — not even coming down for his meals. At the dinner table both the father and the mother barely touched their food. They were thinking of the boy in the attic. Yet, he must be punished; and the father could not conscientiously revoke the punishment. Finally the father excused himself from the table, and made his way up to the attic. When the father entered the room the boy sullenly turned his face to the wall. The father said simply: "Son, I have come to spend the next three days with you."

In what way is Christ our salvation? By being the propitiation for our sins. And what is meant by propitiation? This means that Christ satisfied the wrath of God: that he propitiated the Father by dying on the cross. God, because of his holy nature, could not condone sin. God had pronounced death as the penalty for sin. He therefore could not pardon a sinful man without there being a death for that man's sin. Our sins have been placed on Christ

27

and punishment was meted out on Calvary. God has laid on him the iniquity of us all, and by his stripes we are healed. In the Old Testament the scapegoat foreshadowed what Jesus did on the cross. The sins of the Israelites were ceremonially transferred to the goat, after which the priest could pronounce them clean. In like manner our sins were transferred to Christ. God can therefore forgive us without violating his own righteousness.

> Jesus paid it all, all to him I owe.
> Sin had left a crimson stain
> He washed it white as snow.

Here is the most humbling thought in Scripture. Christ, who lived a sinless life, died as a sinner in order to atone for the sins of the elect. This gives meaning to his words in the Garden of Gethsemane and from the cross. For our Lord to have begged to be delivered from the cross itself would have contradicted his own statements to the effect that he came into the world for the specific purpose of dying (John 12:27). No, Jesus did not ask to be delivered from the *pain* of the cross. Rather he shuddered at the thought of that fleeting period of time when he must assume the role of a sinner. This was what caused him to sweat as it were great drops of blood and to plead "Let this cup pass from me." For the space of time on the cross that Jesus voluntarily took on the role of sinner (sinbearer), God's face was withdrawn from him. Hear his words, "My God, my God, why hast thou forsaken me?"

The prophets had foretold that Messiah would be counted as a sinner in order to become the sinbearer. "Yet it pleased Jehovah to bruise him; he hath put him to grief: when thou shalt make his soul an offering for sin, he shall see his seed, he shall prolong his days, and the pleasure of Jehovah shall prosper in his hand. He shall see of the travail of his soul and shall be satisfied: by the knowledge of himself shall my righteous servant justify many; and he shall bear their iniquities. Therefore will I divide him a portion with the great, and he shall divide the spoil with the strong; because he poured out his soul unto death, and was numbered with the transgressors: yet he bare the sin of many, and made intercession for the transgressors" (Isaiah 53:10-12).

Jesus' sacrificial death was no last minute whim on God's part. Even before he created the world, God anticipated man's need of redemption and foreordained the cross of Christ. And Christ — as an equal member of the Trinity — agreed to this plan. A poet has well said that if one could look into the heart of God he would see there a cross.

Even as God drove Adam and Eve from the garden owing to their sin, he promised that a way of redemption would be opened to man. "And I will put enmity between thee and the woman, and between thy seed and her seed; he shall bruise thy head, and thou shalt bruise his heel" (Gen. 3:15). This has been called the protevangelion. It is the promise that Christ would come into the world, meet Satan on his own ground, and defeat him.

Man's need for salvation was a universal need. "For all have sinned, and come short of the glory of God" (Rom. 3:23). "Therefore, as through one man sin entered into the world, and death through sin; and so death passed unto all men, for that all sinned" (Rom. 5:12). "What then? are we [Jews] better than they [Gentiles]? No, in no wise: for we before laid to the charge both of Jews and Greeks, that they are all under sin; as it is written: There is none righteous, no, not one; There is none that understandeth, There is none that seeketh after God; They have all turned aside, they are together become unprofitable; There is none that doeth good, no, not so much as one: Their throat is an open sepulchre; With their tongues they have used deceit: The poison of asps is under their lips: Whose mouth is full of cursing and bitterness: Their feet are swift to shed blood; Destruction and misery are in their ways; And the way of peace have they not known: There is no fear of God· before their eyes" (Rom. 3:9-18). Compare Romans 11:32.

Sin has been likened to a disease, and salvation to its remedy. Biblical salvation is a complete cure — from diagnosis, to treatment, to good health. The process begins with our regeneration and ends with our complete glorification in heaven.

Amillenarians hold — as did the church fathers and the Protestant reformers — that there has always been only one plan of salvation. Every person who has ever graced, or who ever will grace, the portals of heaven will have one thing in common with all other citizens of heaven. Each one will have come there only through a childlike faith in the shed blood of Jesus Christ. *There is only one plan of salvation.* Yea, and there has never been another plan. Nor will there *ever* be a different plan.

Let us look at the saints of the Old Testament. How were they saved? Was the plan under which they were saved any different from God's plan of salvation for today? Let us look, through the eyes of that great theologian, Paul, at Abraham's salvation. Paul took painstaking care in showing that Abraham's salvation was exactly like that being accepted by Gentiles of Paul's day. Paul contended that, indeed, all men of all time are saved in the exact same manner. Men of the Old Testament looked forward and accepted the propitiation through Christ on faith while those of the New Testament era accept the finished sacrifice. In the eyes of God, however, all are saved through the same propitiation. "We reckon therefore that a man is justified by faith apart from the works of the law. Or is God the God of Jews only? Is he not the God of Gentiles also? Yea, of Gentiles also: if so be that God is one, and he shall justify the circumcision by faith, and the uncircumcision through faith" (Rom. 3:28-30).

"What then shall we say that Abraham, our forefather, hath found according to the flesh? For if Abraham was justified by works, he hath whereof to glory; but not toward God. For what saith the scripture? And Abraham believed God, and it was reckoned unto him for righteousness. Now to him that worketh, the reward is not reckoned as of grace, but as of debt. But to him that worketh not, but believeth on him that justifieth the ungodly, his faith is reckoned for righteousness. Even as David also pronounceth blessing upon the man, unto whom God reckoneth righteousness apart from works . . ." (Rom. 4:1-6).

"For not through the law was the promise to Abraham or to his seed that he should be heir of the world, but through the righteousness of faith. For if they that are of the law are heirs, faith is made void, and the promise is made of none effect: for the law worketh wrath; but where there is no law, neither is there transgression. For this cause it is of faith, that it may be according to grace; to the end that the promise may be sure to all the seed; not to that only which is of the law, but to that also which is of the faith of Abraham, who is the father of us all (as it is written, A father of many nations have I made thee). . ." (Rom. 4:13-18). Read also Galatians 2:16.

Men today are saved by hearing and believing the kerygma (the good news of Christ's death, burial, and resurrection). Abraham was saved through faith in that same gospel. This was the same gospel which was preached by John the Baptist, by our Lord himself, and by all of the apostles. This gospel was preached, in advance, to Abraham (Gal. 3:8) so that he might be the father of all the righteous (Rom. 4:11). "Even as Abraham believed God, and it was reckoned unto him for righteousness. Know therefore that they that are of faith, the same are sons of Abraham. And the scripture, foreseeing that God would justify the Gentiles by faith, preached the gospel beforehand unto Abraham, saying, In thee shall all the nations be blessed. So then they that are of faith are blessed with the faithful Abraham" (Gal. 3:6-9). See also Hebrews 4:2.

A comparison of Genesis 22:18 with Galatians 3:16 and 3:29 makes clear the fact that Abraham's salvation (as well as the salvation of all who are saved) was through the work of Christ on the cross. "And in thy seed shall all the nations of the earth be blessed; because thou hast obeyed my voice" (Gen. 22:18). Paul speaks of this promise, and says, "Now to Abraham were the promises spoken, and to his seed. He saith not, and to seeds, as of many; but as of one, And to thy seed, which is Christ" (Gal. 3:16).

Having shown that Abraham's salvation came about through faith in Christ, Paul goes on to say that indeed every genuine believer — whether he be Jew or Gentile — is a spiritual descendant of Abraham. "For ye are all sons of God, through faith, in Christ Jesus. For as many of you as were baptized into Christ did put on Christ. There can be neither Jew nor Greek, there can be neither bond nor free, there can be no male and female; for ye all are one man in Christ Jesus. And if ye are Christ's, then are ye Abraham's seed, heirs according to promise" (Gal. 3:26-29).

Paul was inspired to emphasize over and over again that no one ever was saved by the law. The function of the law was to show man his need of salvation. "Because by the works of the law shall no flesh be justified in his sight; for through the law cometh the knowledge of sin" (Rom. 3:20).

Nor is man ever saved by works. "Not of works, that no man should glory" (Eph. 2:9). "For if Abraham was justified by works, he hath whereof to glory; but not toward God. For what saith the scripture? And Abraham believed God, and it was reckoned unto him for righteousness. Now to him that worketh, the reward is not reckoned as of grace, but as of debt. But to him that worketh not, but believeth on him that justifieth the ungodly, his faith is reckoned for righteousness. Even as David also pronounceth blessing upon the man, unto whom God reckoneth righteousness apart from works" (Rom. 4:2-6).

In Romans 4 Paul deals with the question of circumcision — since so many Jews thought this act automatically made them righteous and true descendants of Abraham. Speaking of Abraham's imputed righteousness, Paul asks, and answers, a question concerning circumcision: "How then was it reckoned? when he was in circumcision, or in uncircumcision? Not in circumsion, but in uncircumcision: and he received the sign of circumcision, a seal of the righteousness of the faith which he had while he was in uncircumcision: that he might be the father of all them that believe, though they be in uncircumcision, that righteousness might be reckoned unto them. . ." (Rom. 4:10-11).

Some have thought that James taught salvation by works. However, if this were true, it would constitute a contradiction between Paul and James. No such contradiction exists. The same infallible Holy Spirit inspired both men to write. James spoke (James 2:17, 18), not of how to be saved, but of how faith works. In this he and Paul agreed perfectly. Paul taught the same thing. "For we are his workmanship created in Christ Jesus for good works, which God afore prepared that we should walk in them" (Eph. 2:10). Both James and Paul spoke, on these occasions, of a working faith — not of faith by works. Every genuine faith will result in good works. However, no one is saved by good works. These are the evidence of a saving faith, not the cause of it. The Philippian jailor was in dead earnest when he asked Paul, "What must I do to be saved?" If works were necessary, then Paul shortchanged the seeker. For Paul said "Believe on the Lord Jesus, and thou shalt be saved. . ." (Acts 16:31).

We see then that salvation has never come about through the law, or through circumcision, or through works of any kind. How is man saved? Paul spells it out in numerous ways: "For by grace have ye been saved through faith; and that not of yourselves, it is the gift of God; not of works, that no man should glory" (Eph. 2:8, 9). "But now apart from the law a righteousness of God hath been manifested, being witnessed by the law and the prophets; even the righteousness of God through faith in Jesus Christ unto all them that believe; for there is no distinction; for all have sinned, and fall short of the glory of God; being justified freely by his grace through the redemption that is in Christ Jesus: whom God set forth to be a propitiation through faith, in his blood. . ." (Rom. 3:21-25).

Salvation, says the apostle Paul, is by grace. Grace is unmerited favor with God. No person deserves to be saved. Salvation is a free gift from God to certain individuals. We exercise faith in order to be saved, but even our faith is also a gift of God. Faith is the result of regeneration. Unless the Holy Spirit energizes the sinner, that sinner cannot exercise saving faith. Unregenerate man is not capable of turning to God. Jesus said: "No man can come to me, except the Father that sent me draw him; and I will raise him up in the last day" (John 6:44). This strikes a blow at man's pride, but it is very scriptural. And this view alone gives God the glory for man's salvation.

*Conclusion*

There are three phases of the one salvation — past, present, and future. I was saved at the age of 16, I am being saved each day of my life, and I shall be saved from the wrath that is to come. Yet these are but three phases of the one plan of salvation.

Salvation involves union with Christ. In Christ the believer is prophet, priest, and king. This is why Paul could say that *all things* are ours in Christ. The Christian is an heir of God and a joint-heir with Christ. The Holy Spirit, who is our earnest (down payment, as it were) of salvation, bears witness with our spirit, giving assurance of our salvation. And the sufferings of this life, says Paul, are not even to be compared with what God has in store for his own.

On these distinctives there is complete agreement among amillenarians: God has always had but one plan of salvation, that plan rests only on the finished work of Christ, all men stand in need of salvation, and all who are saved are saved in the exact same way, i.e., only through faith in Jesus Christ.

33

# V

## THE CHURCH

The church's greatest need in any generation is to be herself. This is doubly true in our day. The Christian church simply needs to return to being the church. This calls for a definition. Just what is the church, in the true scriptural sense of the word? The New Testament word *ekklesia* is derived from the Greek compound verb *ek kaleo* meaning to call out. Originally the Greek word *ekklesia* was used in referring to any assembly of people. However, the New Testament writers, following the lead of our Lord himself, sanctified this word and used it to describe only Christian groups. So that in the New Testament sense *ekklesia* (church) describes a called-out group of believers in the Lord Jesus Christ.

*Ekklesia* never refers to an individual — Christian, or otherwise. It always denotes an assembly or group of people. The most common use of the word from which the New Testament word was taken was in reference to public assemblies of citizens, summoned together for the purpose of transacting town business (cf. Acts 19:32, 39, 41). The Septuagint used this word to describe the "congregation of Israel." So that the church is never said to be a called-out individual, but, rather, a group of called-out persons. In fact, most translators take "congregation" and "church" to be synonymous terms.

*Ekklesia* (church) has two New Testament usages, i.e., two aspects of the one true church: (1) the elect of all ages, both in heaven and on earth; and (2) distinct local congregations (churches). The first of these is called, by theologians, the invisible church while the latter is referred to as the visible church. Although every true member of the visible church is *ipso facto* a member of the invisible church, it does not follow that every member of the invisible church is also a member of a visible church. In fact, many members of the invisible church are not members of a visible church. No saint who has died the natural death remains a member of a

34

visible church. These have gone to be with the Lord, which according to Paul, "is far better." They have ceased being members of the church militant, but have joined the ranks of the church triumphant.

It was stated earlier that there are two aspects or usages of the word translated "church" in the New Testament. For some reason many Christians — especially many fundamentalists — shy away from the first named of these. Many, in fact, deny that the Bible even speaks of a universal church which comprises every true believer. These folk would limit the name "church" to a local congregation.

Now it must readily be acknowledged that this word refers to local congregations of believers in the vast majority of times it is used in the New Testament. The word *ekklesia* is used some one hundred ten times in the New Testament; and over ninety of these references are to local churches. However, this does not alter the fact that the New Testament also uses *ekklesia* as a description of all believers both in heaven and on the earth. In some cases the context would allow the word to apply either to the over-all church or to a local church — or to both. In other contexts, however, the word can by no stretch of the imagination be restricted to a local body. Let us examine some examples of this fact.

"And I also say unto thee, that thou art Peter, and upon this rock I will build my church; and the gates of Hades shall not prevail against it" (Matt. 16:18). Here the Lord would definitely seem to be referring to the universal church and not to any local body. Nor is Paul speaking of a local assembly when he states: "And he put all things in subjection under his feet, and gave him to be head over all things to the church, which is his body, the fulness of him that filleth all in all" (Eph. 1:22, 23). The following verses would have less than their full significance if applied to any local body. "Husbands, love your wives, even as Christ also loved the church, and gave himself up for it; that he might sanctify it, having cleansed it by the washing of water with the word, that he might present the church to himself a glorious church, not having spot or wrinkle or any such thing; but that it should be holy and without blemish" (Eph. 5:25-27). Certainly Christ's body is larger than any local congregation; and Paul says that Christ's body is the church. "And he is the head of the body, the church: who is the beginning, the firstborn from the dead; that in all things he might have the preeminence" (Col. 1:18). The writer of Hebrews also speaks of the universal church when he says: ". . . to the general assembly and church of the firstborn who are enrolled in heaven, . . ." (Heb. 12:23).

New Testament references to the local aspect of the church are numerous enough to speak for themselves. Jesus himself is quoted only twice in the Gospels as using the word *ekklesia* (Matt. 16:18 and 18:17). In the latter of these references our Lord taught that an obstinate member ought to be brought before the church. Since it is humanly impossible and inconceivable to bring anyone to trial before the invisible church, our Lord could only be referring to a local congregation. Similarly, it would lead to utter theological confusion if one were to take the great majority of New Testament references and try to apply them to the universal church.

Amillennialists, then, believe in two aspects of the one church — the invisible and the visible. While the New Testament has far more to say about the last named of these two aspects, it nonetheless has much to say about both sides of the coin.

What are some of the differences between the visible and the invisible aspects of the church? The visible church, as has been intimated, is confined to the earth. The invisible church, on the other hand, includes in its membership every genuine believer, both the living and the physically dead. The invisible church is said to be universal while the church visible is made up of local congregations.

We have said of the invisible church that it is universal and includes every believer of every generation. The Apostles' Creed defines the church as "the communion of saints." The Westminster Confession gives the historic Christian definition of the invisible church. "The catholic or universal church, which is invisible, consists of the whole number of the elect that have been, are, or shall be gathered into one, under Christ the head thereof; and is the spouse, the body, the fulness of him that filleth all in all" (XXV.1). The word "catholic" as used in creeds and confessions simply means "universal" and has nothing to do with Roman Catholicism. Many Protestants shy away from the reciting of creeds because of this expression. However, this particular fear is groundless; for the invisible church truly is catholic (universal).

36

The Old Testament records two kinds of promises which God made to national Israel: national promises and spiritual promises. The spiritual promises encompassed every spiritual descendant of Abraham, and were not restricted to national Israel (Gen. 12:3; 22:18; Romans 2:28, 29; 4:17; Eph. 2:11-16; 3:6-9; Phil. 3:3; Col. 2:11). The spiritual promises still are being fulfilled through the church today. Israel's national promises all have been either fulfilled or invalidated because of unbelief. Let us trace some of these fulfillments.

A major promise made to Israel as a nation was with reference to their inheriting the Promised Land, Palestine. Has God fulfilled this promise? Or is it, as some claim, yet to be fulfilled after the second coming of Christ? What saith the scripture? According to clear teachings in the Bible this promise was fulfilled, under the leadership of Joshua, some six hundred years after the promise was given to Abraham. "So Joshua took the whole land, according to all that Jehovah spake unto Moses; and Joshua gave it for an inheritance unto Israel according to their divisions by their tribes. And the land rested from war" (Joshua 11:23). In the passage just quoted the reader will note that Joshua took the land "according to all that Jehovah spake unto Moses." Deuteronomy 1:8 should be read in conjunction with this verse. "Behold, I have set the land before you: go in and possess *the land which Jehovah sware unto your fathers,* to Abraham, to Isaac, and to Jacob, to give unto them and to their seed after them" (Deut. 1:8, italics added).

"So Jehovah gave unto Israel all the land which he sware to give unto their fathers; and they possessed it, and dwelt therein. And Jehovah gave them rest round about, *according to all that he sware unto their fathers*: and there stood not a man of all their enemies before them; Jehovah delivered all their enemies into their hand. And there failed not aught of any good thing which Jehovah had spoken unto the house of Israel; *all came to pass"* (Joshua 21:41-45, italics added).

"Yea, forty years didst thou sustain them in the wilderness, and they lacked nothing; their clothes waxed not old, and their feet swelled not. Moreover, thou gavest them kingdoms and peoples, which thou didst allot after their portions: so they possessed the land of Sihon, even the land of the king of Heshbon, and the land of Og king of Bashan. Their children also multipliedst thou as the stars of heaven, and broughtest them into the land concerning which thou didst say to their fathers, that they should go in to possess it. So the children went in and possessed the land, and thou subduedst before them the inhabitants of the land, the Canaanites, and gavest them into their hands, with their kings, and the peoples of the land, that they might do with them as they would. And they took fortified cities, and a fat land, and possessed houses full of all good things, cisterns hewn out, vineyards, and oliveyards, and fruit-trees in abundance: so they did eat, and were filled, and became fat, and delighted themselves in thy great goodness" (Neh. 9:21-25).

Now the fact that Israel was disobedient (Neh. 9:26ff), refused to follow through on the mopping up operation after Joshua's death, fraternized with the enemy, etc., does not alter the fact that they did inherit and govern "the whole land" (Joshua 11:23), even "the land which Jehovah sware unto their fathers to give them." Nor is this fulfillment altered by the fact that Israel failed to hold the land. For, as will be shown later, these promises were conditional. Read Nehemiah 9:28.

Another national promise was that Israel would be delivered from captivity — that she would return to the land, rebuild the temple, reinstitute the blood sacrifices, and so forth. What of this promise? Is its fulfillment past or future? What saith the scripture? "Now in the first year of Cyrus king of Persia, that the word of Jehovah by the mouth of Jeremiah might be accomplished, Jehovah stirred up the spirit of Cyrus king of Persia, so that he made a proclamation throughout all his kingdom, and put it also in writing, saying, Thus saith Cyrus king of Persia, All the kingdoms of the earth hath Jehovah, the God of heaven, given me; and he hath charged me to build him a house in Jerusalem, which is in Judah. Whosoever there is among you of all his people, his God be with him, and let him go up to Jerusalem, which is in Judah, and build the house of Jehovah, the God of Israel, (he is God,) which is in Jerusalem. And whosoever is left, in any place where he sojourneth, let the men of his place help him with silver, and with gold, and with goods, and with beasts, besides the free-will-offering for the house of God which is in Jerusalem. Then rose up the heads of fathers' houses of Judah and Benjamin, and the priests, and the Levites, even all whose spirit God had stirred to go up to build the house of Jehovah which is in Jerusalem. . ." (Ezra 1:1-5).

Note that Cyrus gave his decree in order that "the word of Jehovah by the mouth of Jeremiah might be accomplished." This is related to the following prediction by Jeremiah: "For thus saith Jehovah, After seventy years are accomplished for Babylon, I will visit you, and perform my good word toward you, in causing you to return to this place. . . . And ye shall seek me, and find me, when ye shall search for me with all your heart. And I will be found of you, saith Jehovah, and I will turn again your captivity, and I will gather you from all the nations, and from all the places whither I have driven you, saith Jehovah; and I will bring you again unto the place whence I caused you to be carried away captive" (Jer. 29:10-14).

Jeremiah predicted (c. 626 B.C.) that Israel would go into captivity, and that after seventy years she would be returned to Palestine. Jerusalem fell to the Babylonians in 586 B.C. However, the actual captivity consisted of three waves, with the first group going into captivity in 606 B.C. Cyrus' decree came in 537-36, so that Jeremiah's seventy years were literally fulfilled. Oh the majesty of God's prophecies and their sure fulfillments!

Following her return to the land of Palestine, Israel rebuilt the temple at Jerusalem. This represented another of God's fulfilled promises to national Israel. One should especially read the books of Ezra and Nehemiah for accounts of this feat. The Jews began the rebuilding process shortly after their return in 536 B.C. Ensuing circumstances caused them to become discouraged and to cease work on the temple. Then, in 520 B.C., God raised up two prophets to stir the people to renewed action. These men were Haggai and Zechariah. Four years later, 516 B.C., the rebuilding of the temple was completed.

Dispensationalists contend that the prophecies concerning the rebuilding of the temple are yet to be fulfilled. What saith the scripture? "Now in the second year of their coming unto the house of God at Jerusalem, in the second month, began Zerubbabel the son of Shealtiel, and Jeshua the son of Josadak, and the rest of their brethren the priests and the Levites, and all they that were come out of the captivity unto Jerusalem, and appointed the Levites, from twenty years old and upward, to have the oversight of the work of the house of Jehovah" (Ezra 3:8). "Now the prophets, Haggai the prophet, and Zechariah the son of Iddo, prophesied unto the Jews that were in Judah and Jerusalem; in the name of the God of Israel prophesied they unto them. Then rose up Zerubbabel the son of Shealtiel, and Jeshua the son of Josadak, and began to build the house of God which is at Jerusalem; and with them were the prophets of God, helping them. . ." (Ezra 5:1,2). "And the elders of the Jews builded and prospered through the prophesying of Haggai the prophet and Zechariah the son of Iddo. *And they builded and finished it, acccording to the commandment of the God of Israel*, and according to the decree of Cyrus, and Darius, and Artaxerxes king of Persia. *And this house was finished on the third day of the month of Adar, which was in the sixth year of the reign of Darius the king*" (Ezra 6:14,15, italics added).

Other scriptures could be cited as concrete proof that Israel's earthly promises have been literally and historically fulfilled. However, anyone who would not accept those listed would not accept any number of others. The scriptural and historical facts are: Israel was led captive into Babylon, *according to the scriptures;* Israel remained in captivity for seventy years, *according to the scriptures;* at the end of seventy years Israel was permitted to return to the land, rebuild the temple, and reinstitute the sacrifices, *according to the scriptures.* The dates for these events — which most Sunday school classes have studied many times — are (1) captivity beginning in 606 B.C.; (2) seventy years of captivity from 606 to 536 B.C.; (3) return to Palestine in 536 B.C.; (4) temple completed in 516 B.C. God's prophecies are sure and their fulfillments certain.

### Conditional Promises to Israel

We stated earlier that God's promises to Israel were conditional. Dispensationalists err greatly in teaching that God, in a sense, gave Israel a blank check drawn on the bank of heaven. They teach that God's promises to national Israel are binding upon God — regardless of what Israel does or does not do. This doctrine is based upon a very shallow interpretation of isolated verses of Scripture.

40

When one collates the Scriptures, comparing scripture with scripture, one finds that each of God's promises has an accompanying condition. In most cases these conditions are spelled out. Occasionally, though, they are simply *understood* or taken for granted. One biblical example of a condition being understood, though not mentioned in the passage itself, is found in the book of Jonah. God says, point blank, "Yet forty days, and Nineveh shall be overthrown" (Jonah 3:4).

There it is. A blanket statement. "Yet forty days, and Ninevah shall be overthrown." No conditions are mentioned in the entire book of Jonah. Yet, Ninevah was not destroyed at the appointed time. Why not? Because the condition was in the mind of God that she would be destroyed *unless she repented.* She met the condition by repenting, and, therefore, God did not destroy Ninevah at the end of forty days.

Some scriptures, when taken completely alone, appear to make unconditional promises; and many erroneous doctrines are built upon these prooftexts. However, when the promises are examined alongside of parallel passages or in the light of known rules of hermeneutics, it becomes obvious that many conditions are merely taken for granted. The promises in question are covenant promises; and a covenant is an agreement between two parties. To say that covenant promises are unconditional is in itself a contradiction of terms. Once either party violates the agreements within a covenant that covenant becomes null and void. God's covenants with Israel are no exception. God promised to do certain things *provided* Israel would do certain things. Among the conditions spelled out to Israel are these: obedience, faithful witnessing, circumcision, and acceptance of Messiah at his first advent.

In Genesis 15:6 we read that Abraham believed God and that this belief (faith) was counted unto him for righteousness. Belief here is a condition (understood). In Genesis 17:9 God definitely laid down a condition before blessing Abraham. And we read in Genesis 26:5 that God renewed the covenant with Isaac *"because* Abraham obeyed my voice and kept my charge. . . ."" The word "because" is significant in this conversation. A simple chart will show that there were two parties to the contract between God and national Israel.

| PROMISES | AND | CONDITIONS |
|---|---|---|
| Gen. 12:2 | | Gen. 12:1 |
| 14:2-8 | | 17:9 |
| 15:5 | | 15:6 |
| 17:4 | | 17:9 |
| 17:10,11 | | 17:14 |
| | | Ex. 13:4,5 |
| Deut. 28:1-14 | | Deut. 28:15 |
| 30:15,16 | | 30:17-19 |
| | | Josh. 8:34 |
| | | 24:20 |
| II Sam. 7 | | II Kings 2:3,4 |
| | | 9:4-9 |
| | | 11:11 |
| | | I Chron. 28:7 |
| II Chron. 7:17, 18 | | II Chron. 7:19-23 |

### Israel and the Messiah

The greatest of all promises to national Israel involved the predicted first advent of Jesus Christ. Paul spoke in a summary manner when he said, in Romans 10:4, that Christ is the end of the law, i.e., that to which the law (and the prophets) pointed. So that by rejecting Christ, who was the end of their law, Israel became "guilty of the whole law," and brought the judgments of God upon her head. Messianic promises in the Old Testament are too well known to need much elaboration here. They reach all the way back to Abraham. (Here we are restricting ourselves to messianic promises given to national Israel; actually, messianic promises go back to Genesis 3:15.) Paul said that all Abrahamic promises headed up in Christ: "Now to Abraham were the promises spoken, and to his seed. He saith not, And to seeds, as of many; but as of one, And to thy seed, which is Christ" (Gal. 3:16). Compare also Genesis 22:18. One of the beautiful promises of Israel's Messiah is found in Genesis, chapter 49. "The sceptre shall not depart from Judah, Nor the ruler's staff from between his feet, Until Shiloh come; And unto him shall the obedience of the peoples be" (Gen. 49:10). Christ was, and is, the only hope of Israel. The crucifixion was Israel's most heinous crime against God.

42

It was at this point — their treatment of the Messiah — that Israel failed the most miserably to keep the conditions laid down in God's promises to her. The Scriptures say, "He came unto his own, and they that were his own received him not" (John 1:11). One of the most heartbreaking pictures in the Bible is the account of our Lord's weeping over Jerusalem's rejection of his proffered love. "O Jerusalem, Jerusalem, that killeth the prophets, and stoneth them that are sent unto her! how often would I have gathered thy children together, even as a hen gathereth her chickens under her wings, and ye would not!" (Matt. 23:37). And one can almost feel the blush on the Master's face as Pilate makes his cutting remark. Cutting because so true! "Pilate answered, Am I a Jew? Thine own nation and the chief priests delivered thee unto me. . ." (John 18:35).

What was the penalty for Israel's failure to meet the conditions laid down by Jehovah, and which climaxed in her heinous treatment of the Messiah? "Jesus saith unto them, Did ye never read in the scriptures, The stone which the builders rejected, the same was made the head of the corner; This was from the Lord, And it is marvellous in our eyes? Therefore say I unto you, The kingdom of God shall be taken away from you, and shall be given to a nation bringing forth the fruits thereof. And he that falleth on this stone shall be broken to pieces: but on whomsoever it shall fall, it will scatter him as dust. And when the chief priests and the Pharisees heard his parables, they perceived that he spake of them. . ." (Matt. 21:42-45). "Behold, your house is left unto you desolate" (Matt. 23:28). God turned her over to her own desires and Christ's blood was upon her head. Whereas the temple had been called "My father's house" before, now it became "your house . . . desolate." God withdrew his presence from Israel as a nation. The Jewish state came to a bitter end in A.D. 70. Nor will national Israel ever again be a fruitful nation. This fact is made obvious by Jesus' curse on the fig tree. "Now in the morning as he returned to the city, he hungered. And seeing a fig tree by the way side, he came to it, and found nothing thereon, but leaves only; and he saith unto it, Let there be no fruit from thee henceforward for ever. And immediately the fig tree withered away" (Matt. 21:18, 19). Most conservative Bible students agree that the fig tree represents national Israel. This being true, then our Lord pronounced a curse upon national Israel and said that she would never again bear fruit. This is in perfect agreement with many other prophecies of the Bible.

What we have just said applies to Israel as a nation. It does not, however, apply to the faithful remnant within Israel. Regardless of what the nation did, God has always had his remnant through whom he continued his true work. It was the remnant alone who kept the covenant and the faith alive. God could say to Elijah that seven thousand had not bowed the knee to Baal; each prophet of God received an audience from the remnant; a remnant remained loyal during the captivity and led the return to the land; a remnant followed Judas Maccabeus; and the faithful remnant accepted the Messiah when he came to earth.

Far too much has been read into John 1:11, leaving no room for .hyperbole or for generality. Although the majority of national Israelites rejected Christ — just as the majority of hearers reject him today — it is not true that *all Israel* refused to believe in him. Nor has God's work ever been contingent upon all Israel accepting his program — that is, all national Israel. Paul dealt specifically with this problem, and concluded by saying: "For what if some were without faith? Shall their want of faith make of none effect the faithfulness of God? God forbid: yea, let God be found true, but every man a liar, . . ." (Romans 3:3,4). "And Isaiah crieth concerning Israel, If the number of the children of Israel be as the sand of the sea, it is the remnant that shall be saved: for the Lord will execute his word upon the earth, finishing it and cutting it short. And, as Isaiah hath said before, Except the Lord of Sabaoth had left us a seed, We had become as Sodom, and had been made like unto Gomorrah" (Rom. 9:27-29). "I say then, Did God cast off his people? God forbid. For I also am an Israelite, of the seed of Abraham, of the tribe of Benjamin. God did not cast off his people which he foreknew. Or know ye not what the scripture saith of Elijah? how he pleadeth with God against Israel: Lord, they have killed thy prophets, they have digged down thine altars: and I am left alone, and they seek my life. But what saith the answer of God unto him? I have left for myself seven thousand men, who have not bowed the knee to Baal. *Even so at this present time also there is a remnant according to the election of grace*" (Rom. 11:1-5, italics added).

When John says that Jesus' own received him not, does this mean Israel in her entirety? Some indeed interpret it this way, then proceed to teach that God postponed his plans for Israel until the second coming of Christ. What saith the scripture? Who were Jesus' earthly followers? Of what nationality were the twelve apostles? And what of the nationality of the seventy? And those in the upper room? And those who were saved on the Day of Pentecost? In fact those many thousands of converts recorded in the book of Acts, before Peter preached to the Gentiles in Cornelius' house? And what nationality of people did God use in writing the entire New Testament? The answer to each question is "Jews, Jews, Jews."

The writer once heard a lecture by a Jewish historian. Interestingly enough, the speaker was not a Christian; however, he had for several years taught in a Jewish seminary, and had made a thorough study of the history of Christianity. This Jewish speaker told our audience of ministerial students that there probably were some two million Jewish converts to Christianity during the first century A.D.

Jesus came unto his own and they that were his own (in nationality only) received him not. However, there is more to the story than this. "But as many [of his own] as received him, to them gave he the right to become children of God, even to them that believe on his name" (John 1:12). Somehow the dispensationalists stop and close their Bible after they have read John 1:11. The very next verse makes it clear that not all of Israel rejected Christ, and that these became his followers *at the first advent*. No nation can thwart God's plans and program. Jesus accomplished everything he came to do at his first advent, just as he will also be successful at his second coming. Nothing was postponed!

Those who were merely fleshly descendants of Abraham did reject the Messiah. But those who were the circumcised in heart — the true remnant of Israel — accepted him, and God built them upon the foundation of the prophets and the apostles.

### Israel and the Church

We come now to study the biblical relationship between national Israel and the Christian church. The historic Christian teaching holds that national Israel was a type or forerunner of the church, and that

45

the church replaced Israel on the Day of Pentecost. This view holds that God made two sets of promises to national Israel — national promises, and spiritual promises. All earthly promises to Israel have been either fulfilled or invalidated because of disobedience. All spiritual promises are being fulfilled through the church, which is made up of Jews and Gentiles alike. The first advent of Christ completed Israel's redemption, and manifested the Israel of God (the church) referred to in Galatians 6:16.

The present aspect of the church was prophesied in the Old Testament. These prophecies were, however, clothed in the language of the Old Testament. W. J. Grier makes a pertinent remark on this point. "If the prophets had spoken of the New Testament Church, not under the figures of Israel of old, but in terms of the New Testament grace and truth, would they have been understood? If they had heralded the glories of Christ's people, not under the figures of the land, the temple, and the sacrifices, but in the richness and fulness of the New Testament language, it would have meant nothing and conveyed nothing to the Old Testament Saints. They could not have borne such excess of light. Let us remember that when Christ did come, it was difficult even for His chosen disciples to understand, and that He said to them, 'I have yet many things to say unto you, but ye cannot bear them now.' Only by things known, such as the land, the temple, and the sacrifices could the prophets picture the unknown" (*The Momentous Event*, pp. 30-31).

Our previous chapter showed from the Scriptures that God has but one plan of salvation. There is also only one *body* of God. This body is made up of every born again individual from both the Old and the New Testaments. God's people were known in the Old Testament as "Israel." The same people, in the New Testament, are known as "the church." As a matter of scriptural fact, these terms are used interchangeably; the church is referred to as "Israel" (Gal. 6:16) while the Old Testament remnant is referred to as "the church" (Acts 7:38). There is at least one other New Testament passage wherein the people of God in the Old Testament are referred to as the church. The writer of Hebrews quotes from Psalm 22:22 and applies these words to the New Testament church as being fulfilled at the first advent of our Lord. "I will declare thy name unto my brethren, In the midst of the congregation [church] will I sing thy praise" (Heb. 2:12). The King James Version renders "congregation" in this verse as "church," and the American Standard Version gives this as a marginal reading.

Although it is off the subject at hand, an interesting side comment might well be made here with reference to the use of the word "brethren" in Hebrews 2:12. Dispensationalists attempt to make the judgment in Matthew 25 a judgment distinct from that, say, in Revelation 20. The Matthew 25 judgment, they contend, is a judgment of the nations. They say that this judgment is not for salvation, but rather to determine who (which nations) will enter the millennial reign. This will be determined, we are told, by how the nations treated the "brethren" of Matthew 25. Now comes the crux of our comment: dispensationalists say these "brethren" are the national Israelites. Hebrews 2:12 is one of the many places where the New Testament writers show that the Christian church members are Christ's brethren.

To return now to our subject, the amillennial belief in one body of Christ, this amillennial doctrine is in perfect agreement with the historic Christian belief. This belief was taught by the primitive church fathers, and the Protestant reformers. *The New Bible Dictionary,* in speaking of the New Testament church in Jerusalem, says: ". . . it saw itself as the elect remnant of Israel destined to find salvation in Zion (Joel ii.32; Acts ii.17ff.) and as the restored tabernacle of David which Jesus himself had promised to build (Acts xv. 17; Mt. xvi. 18). Jerusalem was thus the divinely appointed locale for those who awaited 'the times of restitution of all things' (Acts iii.21). Externally, the group of baptized believers had the character of a sect (Gk. *haeresis*) within Judaism" (p. 229).

Although he himself taught otherwise, the late C. I. Scofield admitted that historical Christian teaching held to the doctrine of one people of God. Writing in the introduction of a book by Lewis Sperry Chafer, he said: "Protestant theology has very generally taught that all the kingdom promises, and even the great Davidic covenant itself, are to be fulfilled through the church" (*The Kingdom in History and Prophecy*, p. 5).

Another such admission comes from John Walvoord, one of today's most vocal exponents of dispensationalism. ". . . the traditional Reformed position as illustrated in Calvin is that the church takes Israel's place as its spiritual successor. Calvin regarded Israel's hope of a future kingdom as without warrant — in fact, he held that this hope was a result of their spiritual blindness imposed as a judgment because of their rejection of Christ. Calvin stated: 'And the folly of the whole nation of the Jews in the present age, in expecting an earthly kingdom of the Messiah, would be equally extraordinary, had not the Scriptures long before predicted that they would thus be punished for their rejection of the gospel' " (*The Millennial Kingdom*, pp. 100-101).

Beginning with the faithful remnant out of national Israel, God added to the church all who were saved through the earthly ministry of Jesus. The New Testament aspect of the church started out as a Jewish body. In fact, Cornelius would seem to have been the first Gentile convert to be added to the church in Jerusalem. Then God raised up the apostle Paul as a missionary to the Gentiles; and many Gentile believers were added to the one olive tree which constituted the one body of God.

Far from representing a change in God's plan this was merely the culmination of his progressive revelation concerning the one true church. ". . . whereby, when ye read, ye can perceive my understanding in the mystery of Christ; which in other generations was not made known unto the sons of men, as it hath now been revealed unto his holy apostles and prophets in the Spirit; to wit, *that the Gentiles are fellow-heirs, and fellow-members of the body, and fellow-partakers of the promise in Christ Jesus through the gospel,* whereof I was made a minister . . . to the intent that now unto the principalities and the powers in the heavenly places might be made known through the church the manifold wisdom of God, according to the eternal purpose which he purposed in Christ Jesus our Lord: in whom we have boldness and access in confidence through our faith in him" (Eph. 3:4-10, italics added).

It is generally agreed that Christ probably spoke Aramaic when he said, "I will build my church." Acting upon this assumption, R. W. Kicklighter makes the following statement: "If such be the case, then Christ probably used the Aramaic equivalent for the Hebrew *qahal* and *ekklesia* in the Septuagint. With these considerations in mind, Hort wrote, 'If we may venture for a moment to substitute the name Israel, and read the words as "on this rock I will build my Israel. . ." we gain an impression which supplies at least an approximation to the probable sense.' " (*What Is the Church?* p. 45).

48

That the Christian church replaced Israel is obvious when one notes that the Jewish-Gentile Christian church of the New Testament is given the same titles which in the Old Testament were given to national Israel. Things equal to the same thing are equal to each other. Old Testament passages such as Exodus 19:6; Hosea 1:10; and Isaiah 61:6 would seem to be addressed to the same people as was I Peter 2:9-10. Indeed they were addressed to one and the same group — except that those addressed in the Old Testament were called Israelites while their successors in the New Testament were referred to as the church. Peter lifts expressions and terms almost bodily from these Old Testament prophecies in addressing the Christian church: "But ye are an elect race, a royal priesthood, a holy nation, a people for God's own possession, that ye may show forth the excellencies of him who called you out of darkness into his marvellous light: who in time past were no people, but now are the people of God: who had not obtained mercy, but now have obtained mercy" (I Peter 2:9, 10).

The church, like our salvation and like the kingdom, is old and at the same time new. In its different aspects or phases, the church can be said to be past, present, and future. Born in the mind of God before the foundation of the world, it came into being in the Garden of Eden with the provision that Christ would come forth, meet Satan on his own ground, and defeat him (Gen. 3:15). Someone has well remarked that while the church perhaps came of age at Pentecost, it certainly was not born there. She had existed long before that, under the names "Israel," "the people of God," "the commonwealth of Israel," and other such names.

Although the church has been in existence since the Garden of Eden, there is a sense in which Jesus established a new church. This is why our Lord could speak in future terms and say "I will build my church," without contradicting Stephen who spoke of the church in the wilderness under Moses. The church of Christ is not new cloth on an old garment. Christ reconstructed the old Israel before establishing his church upon the faith of the remnant in him. This new aspect of the church was contingent upon our Lord's victory over Satan (Matt. 12:29), and upon Christ's ascension and seating at the right hand of the Father on that greater throne of the Greater David, which Peter describes in Acts 2:31 and following verses. Here then is a mystery: the church is old and at the same time new. Jesus brought into being a new manifestation of the eternal body of God's people. Vos speaks of the church form of the kingdom, and this gives brilliant insight into this mystery which, according to Paul, remained locked in the heart and mind of God until it was revealed to the apostles. The church, like the kingdom, has three aspects — past, present, and future. The church today is not as it was in the Old Testament. Nor is it the way it will be in glory when God the Son turns it over, without spot or wrinkle, to God the Father. Yet each phase is but a different aspect or manifestation of the one eternal organism.

Here is divine paradox — that the church could have existed throughout the Old Testament and yet be spoken of by our Lord in a future tense: "I will build my church. . . ." Perhaps a human analogy, though weak, will help to elucidate this great truth. Let us picture an old model car that has been wrecked and is now dented and rusty. Let us imagine this old junk heap being completely overhauled. A new motor is installed, new wiring is added, and the body is pounded out and painted by an expert body man. Here, we could say, is a "new" car. No one would question our meaning even though they knew that it was really the old car made over. So it was with the church which Jesus built upon the foundation of the old Israel. In referring to the future church our Lord no doubt had in mind the church as it would be after he had returned to the Father, there to intercede for the church while seated on the throne of heaven as the exalted head of the church. The future church which our Lord prophesied would look back — as the church indeed does look back today — upon the finished work of Christ on the cross, upon his death, burial, triumph over death, and ascension to the right hand of the Father. This phase of the church so far outshines the church in the wilderness under Moses that it is for all intents and purposes a "new" church. Yet, like the old car in our analogy, it is built upon the frame of the old church, which is Israel.

Paul said that God took two "men" (all believing Israelites plus all believing Gentiles) and made them into one. The church was wed to Israel thus becoming one person even as God weds a woman to a man and the two persons become one in God's sight. Here is divine mystery indeed and it is marvellous in our eyes.

50

Jesus said, "Upon this rock I will build *my* church. . . ." The church truly is his, and he is the only head of the church. ". . . which he wrought in Christ, when he raised him from the dead, and made him to sit at his right hand in the heavenly places, far above all rule, and authority, and power, and dominion, and every name that is named, not only in this world, but also in that which is to come: and he put all things in subjection under his feet, and gave him to be head over all things to the church, which is his body, the fulness of him that filleth all in all" (Eph. 1:20-23).

Rome does great violence to this doctrine, and builds *her* "church" upon the apostle Peter. They base this dogma on Jesus' words to Peter: "And I also say unto thee, that thou art Peter, and upon this rock I will build my church. . ." (Matt. 16:18). Several worthy arguments can be raised to refute this interpretation. In the first place, the genders of the two words are different. Christ addressed Peter as *Petros* [masculine], then said that upon this *petra* [feminine] he would build his church. It also should be noted that Jesus elsewhere gave the keys to the kingdom to all the apostles. Too, Paul says the church is built upon the foundation of all the apostles, and not upon Peter alone (Eph. 2:20).

It is likely that our Lord had one of two things in mind — or perhaps a combination of both of these — when he uttered the words in Matthew 16:18: (1) his church would be built upon Peter's confession, which acknowledged Jesus as the Christ, the Son of the living God; or (2) since Peter spoke as a representative for all the apostles, this ties in with Paul's statement that the church is built upon the foundation of the prophets and apostles. Matthew 16:15 makes it clear that the question, "Who say *ye* that I am?" was directed to all the apostles. Peter answered for the group.

At any rate the church is obviously not built upon Peter alone. It is built upon all those who had Peter's kind of faith in the lordship of Christ. Christ himself is the chief cornerstone and every believer is a building block in that holy temple (Eph. 2:22).

> The church's one foundation
> Is Jesus Christ her Lord;

She is His new creation
  By Spirit and the Word
From heaven He came and sought her
  To be His holy bride,
With His own blood He bought her,
  And for her life He died.

It was revealed to John that the Lord walks in the midst of his churches (Rev. 1:13). This was equally true of the church in the Old Testament, according to the apostle Paul: ". . . for they drank of a spiritual rock that followed them: and the rock was Christ" (I Cor. 10:4). Christ loved his church and gave himself for it, purchasing her with his shed blood (Eph: 5:1, 25).

The church is not Christ, but it is his body. The church is to Christ what the body is to the head. The church is not her own, she is bought with a price. Therefore the church is submissive to the commands of Christ.

*The Church is Holy*

Before any local congregation can exemplify the true church, that local body must meet at least four requirements: (1) a regenerate membership, (2) separated lives on the part of its members, (3) correct doctrine, and (4) faithful administration of the two church ordinances — baptism and the Lord's Supper. A chapter would be required to cover any one of these four requirements. But, since these are central points in an examination of amillennialism, let us look at least briefly at each requirement.

The Scriptures say that without holiness no man shall see the Lord (Heb. 12:14). The Apostles' Creed speaks of the holy catholic church. Amillennialists believe in the *holy* catholic (universal) church because it is taught in the Scriptures. The *ground* of this holiness is the Head of the church, Jesus Christ himself. The *basis* of the holiness of the church is her regenerate membership. Only the twice-born ones belong to the true church. God alone can add members to his church, and he restricts membership to those who have been cleansed by the washing of regeneration.

Is there scriptural proof for insisting that only regenerated persons are members of the true church of God? John the Baptist, the forerunner of Christ, who set the stage for the church, laid down this requirement. Those who came to John for baptism were told that they must first show evidence of repentance (Matt. 3:8). This indicates clearly that John would baptize only believers, i.e., those who repented of sin and publicly acknowledged Jesus as Savior and Lord. Luke informs us in the Acts that each of the three thousand people who were added to the church on the Day of Pentecost had heard the gospel preached by Peter, had believed this gospel, and had been baptized upon a profession of their faith in what Peter preached, i.e., Christ. "They then that received his word were baptized: and there were added unto them in that day about three thousand souls" (Acts 2:41). Philip, the evangelist, came upon a man who was reading from Isaiah 53. Philip joined the man in his chariot, and preached unto him Jesus (Acts 8:35)—basing his sermon upon Isaiah 53. Having heard the gospel, the Ethiopian eunuch requested baptism. However, Philip would not baptize the man until he first expressed his faith in Christ. "And Philip said, If thou believest with all thine heart, thou mayest. And he answered and said, I believe that Jesus Christ is the Son of God. And he commanded the chariot to stand still: and they went down both into the water, both Philip and the eunuch; and he baptized him" (Acts 8:37, 38, KJV). Though there is some question as to whether or not verse 37 was in the original manuscripts, Bible scholars believe this was a formula which was asked of all candidates for baptism by the primitive church.

Scriptures like the above could be quoted almost at random to prove that only believers were permitted to follow the Lord in baptism, thus illustrating that the true church was made up of a regenerate membership.

Amillennialists believe that in order for the church to "play the part" her members must live a separated life. Christians are to be in the world, but not of the world. The separated (holy) life is the opposite of worldliness. The professing church has lost the respect of sinners because far too many Christians have lost sight of their calling and have been pressed into the mold of things about them.

We need to be reminded that the church is a called-out organism. In the church of the Old Testament, Israel was called out from the rest of the sons of men to do special service for God — to be his peculiar people. The New Testament church also is called out from the world. And if the church has been called out *from* something, it has also been called *to* something, i.e., to holy living that God may be glorified in her actions. Paul instructs every Christian to put off the deeds of the old man and to put on Christ.

We stated that the church must have correct doctrine. What constitutes correct doctrine? The scriptural answer to this question lies in a study of the primitive churches along with the instructions given them in the epistles. One of the outstanding characteristics of the first church members is found in the second chapter of the Acts. "And they continued stedfastly in the apostles' teaching and fellowship, in the breaking of bread and the prayers" (Acts 2:42). The King James Version used the word "doctrine" where the American Standard Version uses the word "teaching." In this case they are synonymous terms, since a doctrine is a *teaching* of the church.

When we read in this verse that they continued stedfastly in the apostles' doctrine, we gain the mental picture of something being held onto tenaciously. And this is a correct picture of what the early church did. They gave up their homes, their families, yea, and even their lives rather than surrender one article of this doctrine.

How present-day professing Christians have surrendered this determination to follow in the apostles' doctrine! The attitude of the World Council of Churches holds sway today. The council plays on two strings: church union is played on the high string while doctrine is played on the low one. To put it another way, the Council of Churches plays up church union and plays down doctrine. Since strong convictions on any given doctrine would stand in the way of church union — and since church union is a god they have come to worship — the council leaders say that doctrine is not important. The reason for this lies primarily in the fact that these men do not accept the Bible as the infallible Word of God. They have, at the most, a fragmented, truncated Bible. There are no absolutes in their systems. Everything is relevant, and, therefore, man's reasoning power has the final say on every subject.

"They continued stedfastly in the apostles' teaching [doctrine]." What exactly is meant by the apostles' teaching? Did it originate in the minds of the apostles? In actuality, the apostles' doctrine is none other than Christ's doctrine. Before Jesus instructed them to "go preach," he called them to "come, follow me." These men had the unique privilege of studying in the finest seminary the world has ever known anything about. For three and one half years their classrooms ranged from a boat, to a field, to a cave, to borrowed rooms. Their teacher was the Lord of heaven — God, walking in the form of man.

As the earthly ministry of our Lord was drawing to its planned close, he said to his disciples that they were to go everywhere making disciples; and they were to teach these disciples "to observe all things whatsoever I commanded you. . ." (Matt. 28:20). We see then that the apostles' doctrine was in reality Christ's doctrine, and that they were instruments through which he proclaimed this doctrine after his death. Paul, who perhaps did more than any other man in formulating the apostles' doctrine into a systematic theology, could say humbly: "For I determined not to know anything among you, save Jesus Christ, and him crucified" (I Cor. 2:2).

It is expedient, in these days of doctrinal laxness, that the visible church study to show herself approved *unto God*. It is expedient that we return to the apostles' doctrine, then continue *stedfastly* in it. This would do more than any other one thing to revive the present-day churches. For without doctrinal purity it is impossible to meet the other three requirements — a regenerate membership, separated living, and faithful administration of the church ordinances.

The Roman Catholic Church has formulated seven sacraments which their priests must perform. These are: baptism, eucharist, confirmation, orders, matrimony, penance, and extreme unction. They claim saving efficacies for these so-called sacraments. Protestants, on the other hand, accept only those rites found in Scripture —baptism, and the Lord's Supper. Some Protestants have followed Rome in placing degrees of saving efficacies on these, although most Protestants prefer to think of them as outward signs of inward graces. Many Protestants in fact prefer to use the term "ordinances," thus staying away from the connotation Rome has attached to the word "sacrament." Neither term is laid down by the New Testament, although the word "ordinance" is used many times in Scripture referring to God's statutes, customs, commands, traditions, or to things prescribed by statutes.

*Conclusion*

The Christian church is by definition a group of called-out believers. The invisible church is made up of all the saints of all time, both those who are alive today and those who sleep in Jesus. The visible aspect of the church is made up of distinct local congregations of believers. It is well to emphasize that these are not two separate churches, but, rather, two aspects of the one true church.

National Israel was a type of the Christian church. God made conditional promises to Israel. She failed to meet these conditions, and God justifiably turned to the Gentiles. The Christian church was prophesied in the Old Testament — in Old Testament language and Old Testament figures. The fulfillment came, however, in New Testament terms.

The church existed in the Old Testament in the form of the elect remnant within national Israel. Israel was the type while the Christian church is the antitype or fulfillment. Christ, by dying on the cross, tore down the middle wall of partition, took the two men — Israelites and Gentiles — and made the two into one man thus constituting the body of Christ. (Eph. 2:14-16). Though the mystery was hidden from the Old Testament prophets in general, it was God's plan all along to include Gentile believers in the body of which the believing remnant of Israel was the human foundation. (Eph. 3:4-6).

The church actually has three phases or forms — past, present, and future. The New Testament refers to Israel as the church in the wilderness, while it refers to the Christian church in terms unmistakenly reserved heretofore for national Israel. Jesus' actual presence, and his finished work on Calvary, built a *new* church. Yet, it was new only in the sense of being completely renewed and improved. For God has but one body. Following the second coming of Christ, the church will be improved even more and in that sense will again represent a "new" church. For then its members will all be united in glory, their glorified bodies will then match their already redeemed souls (Romans 8:23), the earth will have been cleansed and renewed, and the one true church will reign with Christ in the new heavens and the new earth.

# VI

## ESCHATOLOGY

Amillenarians believe the Lord, at his first advent, set eschatology in motion. He ushered in the last days. The first advent and the second coming of Christ complement each other. They are two parts of one whole. One is incomplete without the other. All things or events set in motion by the first advent will be consummated at the second coming.

Amillenarians believe there is more "realized eschatology" than the millenarians are willing to admit. We also believe, however, that much remains to be fulfilled in matters of eschatology. Jesus ushered in the kingdom age predicted in the Old Testament; though that kingdom is growing progressively toward its consummation, it yet remains to be perfected. Jesus brought judgment upon the world; he brings continued judgments upon the world — judgments such as the fall of Jerusalem in A.D. 70, the fall of Rome in A.D. 476, etc.; yet a final judgment awaits the world at the end of time. Jesus brought salvation to his own; his own are being saved continuously; yet the consummation of that salvation awaits his second coming, the resurrection, and the final rewarding of his saints into their glorified states. In this chapter we shall deal in scriptural detail with these and other aspects of eschatology.

Although amillenarians disagree among themselves on other doctrines, they present a united front with reference to eschatology. The amillennial teachings here are clear and orderly on all basic points. We believe essentially the following order of events constitutes New Testament eschatological teaching: (1) At his first advent our Lord met Satan on his own ground and, in fulfillment of scriptures such as Genesis 3:15, defeated Satan. Satan now lives on probation until the second coming. In the meantime his power is definitely limited, especially in regards to God's people. (2) Having bound Satan, our Lord ushered in the millennial kingdom of Revelation 20. This millennium commenced at the first advent and will end at the second coming, being replaced by the eternal state. (3) Though God presently reigns in the hearts of his people (spiritual Israel), the church was forewarned by her Lord that she would face tribulation so long as she remains on the earth. This tribulation will grow progressively worse until it finally culminates in the appearance of the antichrist. While God has cautioned his people that tribulation would be their lot, he also has promised to protect them through every persecution they must face. The church militant is assured of becoming the church triumphant. (4) Satan, who is now bound in one aspect of his power, will be restored to complete power for a short period of time. This loosing of Satan will come near the end of the present millennium, and he will be put down by the second coming of Christ. (5) The Lord will appear the second time in a literal bodily manner. This coming will bring to completion everything set in motion at the first advent. At this second coming, Satan will be cast into hell. (6) At the second coming there will be a general resurrection of all the dead of all time. (7) This will be followed immediately by a general judgment, resulting in the final separation of the righteous and the wicked. The saints will be present, but will be judged only to ascertain their rewards since their salvation has already been decided. (8) The earth will be cleansed and purified by fire. (9) The eternal state pictured in Revelation 21 and 22 will become a reality, and will last forever. (10) All saints of all time will reign in this eternal state, glorifying God, throughout eternity. The wicked will spend eternity in hell. Briefly stated, this is the amillennial belief on eschatology. Let us now treat these events in scriptural detail.

### Satan is Bound and Doomed

What is meant by the binding of Satan? When John speaks, in Revelation 20, of Satan being bound for a thousand years — does John mean that there will be a period of time during which Satan is completely immobilized? Does being bound, in the scriptural sense, mean that Satan would be so trussed that he could no longer oppose God? or that he could no longer go about like a roaring lion?

Premillenarians have read more into this figure than the Scriptures will allow. The binding of Satan fixes a false image in the minds of many people. So much so that when someone suggests that Satan is bound today these people immediately think this suggestion borders on the edge of lunacy. How, they ask incredulously, can anyone look about him at all the evil workings of Satan and yet say that Satan is bound! Can a being that is bound and cast into a bottomless pit commit such acts?

The correct answer to the above questions depends on just what is depicted by the binding of Satan. If his being bound means that he cannot move a muscle against God then the answer is obvious: he most certainly is not bound today. If he were bound in this literal sense then the earthly utopia looked for by the millenarians would be upon us. If, on the other hand, Satan's binding refers (in figurative language) to the limiting of his power, then he could well be bound already.

What saith the scripture? (1) Satan was bound at the first advent, and (2) Satan still goes about like a roaring lion seeking whom he may devour. Satan is the archenemy of God and he is the ultimate cause of every sin and trouble. These are not contradictory statements. Both are taught in the New Testament.

Do we have scriptural proof that our Lord has already bound Satan? "But if I by the Spirit of God cast out demons, then is the kingdom of God come upon you. Or how can one enter into the house of the strong man, and spoil his goods, except he first bind the strong man? and then he will spoil his house" (Matt. 12:28, 29).

Satan is alluded to in Scripture as the prince of this world. In Matthew 12, our Lord plays upon this phrase when he says that his miracles prove two things: (1) the kingdom of God had arrived, and (2) he had bound the strong man of the house (this world). Otherwise, our Lord asked the critical Pharisees, how could these miracles be performed on Satan's own territory unless Satan had indeed been bound and could therefore not prevent the working of miracles? It is difficult to see how any student of the Bible could miss the import of the conversation between Jesus and his critics there in Matthew 12:22-37.

This writer looked up the Greek meaning of the word "bind" used by our Lord in Matthew 12:29. He found that this word and

59

the word "bound," which is used in Revelation 20:2, are from one and the same root word in the Greek. Any interested reader may turn to these two words, and he will learn that the lexicons refer him to the same source for both. Strong's *Greek Dictionary of the New Testament* lists both of these words under 1210. There one reads: "1210. deo; a prim. verb; to bind (in various applications, lit. or fig): — bind, be in bonds, knit, tie, wind. . ." (p. 21).

Strong informs us then that the word "bind" (or "bound") may be used in either a literal or a figurative sense in the New Testament. This is the very important point which is overlooked by the premillenarian. He can conceive only of a literal binding of Satan.

In cases where the Bible allows more than one meaning for a given word, the context must determine which of the meanings is intended. In this case our Lord himself said that he bound Satan. Yet we know that Satan was not literally bound to the extent that he became immobile. Therefore the context tells us that Jesus spoke of a figurative binding. The context of Revelation 20:2 also tells us that John spoke in the same manner. For a spiritual being cannot be bound with a literal chain or locked with a literal key. Yet John spoke in terms of binding with a chain and a key.

Nor are these the only places where the New Testament uses this term "bound" in a figurative sense. Paul uses this word in a figurative sense many places. "And now, behold, I go bound in the spirit unto Jerusalem, not knowing the things that shall befall me there. . ." (Acts 20:22). Here Paul said that he was "bound," and he used the same word found in Revelation 20:2 and Matthew 12:29. It goes without saying that the context leaves no doubt as to whether or not Paul was immobilized by this binding.

"For the woman that hath a husband is bound by law to the husband while he liveth. . ." (Rom. 7:2). "Art thou bound unto a wife? seek not to be loosed. Art thou loosed from a wife? seek not a wife" (I Cor. 7:27). Here Paul speaks of marriage as a binding together of a man and a woman. Yet think of all the freedom of movement and freedom of action enjoyed by both the husband and the wife. To be bound does not indicate immobility in all cases. Soldiers are bound to their country, men are bound to their chosen professions. Still, all of these enjoy much freedom of movement. So it is with Satan: He is bound, yet he has freedom of movement and is free to tempt, debauch, and ruin lives in spite of this binding. (1 Peter 5:8, 9; Eph. 2:2; 6:12).

The first advent in general, and the death, burial, and resurrection in particular, bound Satan, and he has been a doomed foe ever since. He is now under a suspended sentence. He goes about like a roaring lion *because he knows that his time is short* (Rev. 12:12). When Christ returns the second time to the earth he will then execute the sentence which has already been irrevocably pronounced upon Satan.

The binding of Satan is definitely tied in with the cross of Christ. Jesus was looking toward the crucifixion when he said, "Now is the judgment of this world: now shall the prince of this world be cast out. And I, if I be lifted up from the earth, will draw all men unto myself. But this he said, signifying by what manner of death he should die" (John 12:31-33). These verses should be studied alongside of Revelation 12. For in that chapter of the Revelation John records how that Christ defeated Satan at the first advent and how Satan then turned his wrath upon the church, which he continues to persecute.

The writer of Hebrews says that Christ, through his death, brought to nought (rendered helpless) the power of Satan. ". . . that through death he might bring to nought him that had the power of death, that is, the devil" (Heb. 2:14).

Paul also refers to the cross as the means by which Satan's power was limited, i.e., through which Satan was bound. "Having despoiled the principalities and the powers, he made a show of them openly, triumphing over them in it" (Col. 2:15). ". . . when he ascended on high, he led captivity captive. . ." (Eph. 4:8).

John says, "To this end was the Son of God manifested, that he might destroy the works of the devil" (I John 3:8). We have already mentioned John's treatment of this same subject in Revelation 12. Here one recalls the words of our Lord to the seventy, "And he said unto them, I beheld Satan fallen as lightning from heaven" (Luke 10:18). Here again our Lord made reference to the impending crucifixion.

Having shown from Scripture that Satan already has been bound, in a figurative sense, let us see how this squares with Revelation 20:2. After all, this is the only passage in dispute concerning the alleged future binding of Satan. The question arises, then, whether John meant to portray a literal binding or a figurative one? If he speaks of a literal binding, indicating that Satan will be completely immobilized so that he can carry on no activities at all, then our dispensational friends are correct; this would mean that the predicted binding of Satan has not yet taken place.

If, on the other hand, John spoke of a figurative binding of Satan the problem dissolves itself. For we have shown conclusively that Satan is bound in this manner. Let us get the passage before us.

"And I saw an angel coming down out of heaven, having the key of the abyss and a great chain in his hand. And he laid hold on the dragon, the old serpent, which is the Devil and Satan, and bound him for a thousand years, and cast him into the abyss, and shut it, and sealed it over him, that he should deceive the nations no more, until the thousand years should be finished: after this he must be loosed for a little time" (Rev. 20:1-3).

It should be borne in mind that the Bible often uses the word "bind" to designate the limitation of power. This is the sense in which John uses the term here as the context bears out. John definitely is speaking in figurative language since a spiritual being (Satan) certainly could not be bound with physical keys, chains, and the like. John says that Satan is bound in a particular respect, i.e., "that he should deceive the nations no more." This is the only sense in which this passage says that Satan is bound. In other words, it merely says that one portion of his power has been limited for a period of time.

To understand what is meant by Satan's inability any longer to deceive the nations one merely needs to let his mind take a cursory glance at the teachings of the Bible. In the beginning God placed man in the Garden of Eden and gave man dominion over the earth. At the fall of man in the Garden, Satan took over this dominion from man and became the prince of this world. Even at that time God promised that his Son would some day take this dominion away from Satan (Gen. 3:15).

Before our Lord defeated Satan at the cross, Satan was able to "deceive the nations |Gentiles|" and to hold sway over their souls. On the cross our Lord said, "It is finished." Then and there Satan had this world's dominion wrested from his grasp. He can no longer deceive the nations by keeping the gospel from them. Following his victory on the cross our Lord could say, ". . . all authority hath been given unto me in heaven and on earth. Go ye therefore, and make disciples of all the nations. . ." (Matt. 28:18, 19). Satan's power to deceive the nations had been limited, *because all authority had been given unto Christ.*

## The Millennium

The only place in the entire Bible where the millennium is mentioned per se is in Revelation 20. Still, this lone passage probably has generated more theological arguments than has any other single passage from the Bible. Millennial beliefs have developed until actually there are now five separate schools of thought on the subject. Another of my books* treats all five of these theories. Space here will permit us to deal briefly with only three broad views — premillennialism, postmillennialism, and amillennialism. Since the main emphasis of this work is amillennialism naturally more space will be devoted to this school. The others are brought in only to form a basis for comparison. All three groups definitely believe in a millennium. They differ, however, concerning the *kind* of millennium Revelation 20 describes, and the *time* of that millennium.

Premillenarians teach that Christ will return before (pre) the millennium. At the second coming of Christ only the Christian dead will be resurrected. These along with living Christians will be caught up to meet the Lord in the air. This is called the rapture of the church. Following this "first resurrection" the millennium will be established on the earth. This will be a one thousand year period during which Satan is bound, and during which perfect righteousness will prevail on the earth. The saints will reign with Christ throughout this period. He will reign from Jerusalem where he will be seated on the throne of David in a rebuilt temple. This is but a brief description of premillennialism and does not take into account the "secret rapture," alleged seven-year period, postponement theories, superiority of the Jews during the millennium, etc., which beliefs are held by many present-day premillenarians.

Postmillenarians teach that Christ will not return until after (post) the millennium. Before the second coming the gospel will have

*William E. Cox, *Biblical Studies in Final Things*, Presbyterian and Reformed Publishing Co., Philadelphia, Pa.

so permeated the world that almost the entire population will have been saved. They expect the world to become better and better until the millennium is ushered in. The millennium will be a period during which a truly Christian government will be established all over the world, with most governors, presidents, etc., being genuine Christians, with a high degree of justice prevailing. There will then be a near-perfect reign of peace and prosperity. Satan will be bound during this period.

Amillennialism literally means "no millennium." This is an unfortunate term, however, since amillenarians definitely do believe in a millennium based on Revelation 20:1-10. They simply rebel against the hyperliteralism placed on this passage by the millennialists. Amillenarians interpret Revelation 20:1-10 as representing the period of time between the two advents of our Lord, that is, as going on at the present time and ending when our Lord returns. They equate the millennium with the church age. In other words, whereas other millennialists place a literal interpretation upon Revelation 20:1-10, thus gaining an earthly, material kingdom, amillenarians interpret this passage in a spiritual manner, believing it to be figurative language describing the spiritual reign of Christ in the hearts of his people, which already is going on. Amillenarians would be like the postmillenarian in that both believe the millennium precedes the second coming of Christ. They would be like the premillenarian in that both believe good and evil will exist side by side until the end of the world.

Amillenarians base their millennial doctrine on two basic facts: (1) the nature of the book of Revelation, and (2) the clear teaching of other scriptures relating to the subject matter of Revelation 20.

The only mention of the one thousand year reign is couched in the twentieth chapter of the most figurative book in the Bible. It seems strange indeed that so many people would begin here and build the main basis of all their teachings on this one obscure passage. The word "millennium" is not actually mentioned anywhere in Scripture. Our word "millennium" is based on two Latin words: *mille,* meaning thousand, and *annum,* meaning year. John does speak, in Revelation 20:1-10, of a one thousand year period, i.e., a millennium.

It needs to be emphasized over and over again that the arguments are not as to whether or not the Bible speaks of a millennium.

The only arguments revolve around the interpretation one places upon the scriptures which describe this millennium. Amillenarians refuse to let this one obscure passage govern the entire Bible. Since the passage itself gives no explanation of John's meaning, its meaning must be garnered elsewhere in the Bible.

That the book of Revelation is a book of symbols and figures of speech should bear no argument. Apocalyptic writings are known to have certain definite characteristics, such as figurative language, imagery, numerology, hyperbole, and the like. These are used for a purpose — to teach spiritual lessons to God's people. The numerology, imagery, etc., are not meant to be ends within themselves. Rather they are to be only means to an end, i.e., to get across the central truth God has for his people. The figurative language of the Bible is nonetheless true, as is every word of Scripture.

In the opening verse of the book of Revelation John is told that the information would be *signified* to him. This word means just what the syllables say: sign-i-fied. The Greek word "signify" means to speak in sign language, to make use of symbols, numerology, figures of speech, and so forth. Why should John suddenly change his style once he nears the end of the book? Why should it seem strange that the twentieth chapter would still be *signifying* when it deals with the binding of Satan, and with the millennial reign of Christ with his saints? The amillenarian believes John is still signifying, i.e., making use of symbols and figures of speech while describing the present church age during which Jesus Christ reigns in the hearts of his saints. In John's mind, the one thousand years represented a perfect period of time the end of which is known only to God.

We stated earlier that amillenarians reached their conclusions on the millennium by comparing Revelation 20 with the clear passages of Scripture. There is a very important rule of hermeneutics which states that the obscure passages should always be governed by the clear passages. No clear passage of Scripture anywhere speaks of an earthly, materialistic millennium like the one put forth by the millenarians. As a matter of fact, their alleged millennium militates against many clear passages of the Bible. The Scriptures outline but two ages: the present age and the age to come. The age to come is everywhere said to be eternal, and would therefore be in complete contradistinction to an interregnum of one thousand years.

*The Millennium and the Kingdom of God*

One very important fact seems to escape the attention of most people. This is the fact that millenarians equate the millennium with the kingdom of God. They also equate it with the golden age prophesied in the Old Testament. It is this latter fact which causes them to insist upon a literal, material millennium. They apply a hyperliteral interpretation to the prophecies referring to the golden age, and insist that it must be situated in earthly surroundings before the eternal state is ushered in.

Amillenarians also equate the millennium with the kingdom of God. However, they equate the golden age with the eternal state. Their system therefore does not call for a hyperliteral interpretation of the passages in question. They find it easy to believe that the kingdom of God and/or the millennial reign is a present reality.

We shall deal later with the golden age. At this point, let us nail down our assertion that each school of millennial thought — and this includes amillenarians — says the kingdom of God and the millennium are one and the same thing. This teaching has great significance regarding biblical eschatology. To prove that one exists is to prove *ipso facto* that the other also is a present reality.

"Premillennialism is that view of the Last Things which holds that the second coming of Christ will be followed by a period of world-wide peace and righteousness, before the end of the world, called *'the millennium'* or *'the kingdom of God'* during which Christ will reign as King in person on this earth" (J. G. Vos, *Blue Banner Faith and Life,* Oct.-Dec., 1949, p. 149, italics added).

The above quotation from Prof. Vos shows conclusively that premillenarians equate the kingdom of God with the millennial reign of Christ on the earth.

Clarence Larkin, who for years has been a leading spokesman for the dispensational school of thought, specifically states that the kingdom and the millennium are synonymous terms: "By Pre-Millennial we mean before the Millennium. That is, before the period of a 'Thousand Years' spoken of in Rev. 20:1-6. This period is spoken of in glowing terms by the prophets as a time when the earth shall be blessed with a universal rule of righteousness. . ." (*Dispensational Truth,* p. 10).

That dispensationalists look on the millennium as being synonymous with the kingdom of God is again seen in the writings of Lewis Sperry Chafer. Chafer taught that: (1) The kingdom was predicted by the prophets as a glorious kingdom for Israel on earth when the messianic Son of David would sit on David's throne and rule over the nations from Jerusalem. (2) The kingdom was announced by John the Baptist, Christ, and the apostles. The gospel of the kingdom (Matt. 4:23; 9:35) and the proclamation that the kingdom of heaven was at hand (Matt. 3:2; 4:17) consisted of a legitimate offer to Israel of the promised earthly Davidic kingdom, designed particularly for Israel. However, the Jewish nation rejected their King and, with him, the kingdom. (3) Because of Israel's rejection, the kingdom was postponed until the second advent of Christ. The millennial kingdom was offered, and postponed; but it will be instituted on earth after Christ's return.

Here, then, is the gist of much millennial thinking today: Christ offered to Israel a kingdom. This proffered kingdom was to have been an earthly messianic reign, patterned after David's kingdom of the Old Testament. The throne of David was to have been set up in the temple at Jerusalem, where Jesus was to rule with a rod of iron — forcing saved and unsaved alike to worship him and to perform the rituals and sacrifices performed in the Old Testament temple. Israel was to have had a chosen place of authority during this kingdom (millennial) reign. One cannot help but see the great similarity between these teachings and the beliefs of those unbelieving Jews who put Jesus on the cross for not satisfying their material misconceptions of just such a kingdom.

Amillenarians rebel against the crass materialism of such a proposed kingdom with Christ as its head. Our Lord had many opportunities to head up just such a kingdom during his earthly reign. However, he flatly refused these offers to make him an earthly king, stating that his was not such a kingdom as this.

If amillenarians rebel against the crass materialism and the hyperliteralism of the millennialists, they abhor even more so the Christological implications of these teachings and their implications for the means of salvation.

Assuming, for the sake of argument, that our Lord did offer an earthly Davidic kingdom and that this kingdom was rejected and then postponed — does this not logically indicate that our Lord failed at his first advent to accomplish what he came into the world to do? If the Lord wanted to establish an earthly kingdom, and if he attempted to do so but failed, then one's Christology goes begging. A person holding such a Christology as this is a liberal theologian, regardless of what title he might choose for himself!

The amillenarian honors his Lord by teaching that the Son of God accomplished every work he came to do, and that he shall never fail in any undertaking.

And what of the plan of salvation, if this theory were correct? Let us assume that our Lord had not failed in his attempt to establish an earthly kingdom? What if the unbelieving Jews had not been able to thwart Jesus' plan? what then? The implication here is astoundingly simple: the cross would then not have been necessary. People would have been saved by offering the prescribed animal sacrifices and by keeping the law of Moses. Leading dispensational writers unblushingly advocate this teaching.

"It can be said at once that His dying was not God's own plan. It was conceived somewhere else and yielded to by God. God has a plan of atonement by which men who were willing could be saved from sin and its effect.

"That plan is given in the Old Hebrew code. To the tabernacle or temple, under prescribed regulations, a man could bring some animal which he owned. The man brought that which was his own. It represented him" (S. D. Gordon, *Quiet Talks About Jesus,* p. 114). This book, along with *The Scofield Reference Bible,* has done more to influence dispensational thought than any other piece of literature. Yet this author taught that the cross of Christ was a mere afterthought, being secondary to animal sacrifices.

Lewis Sperry Chafer lends his great influence to this same teaching. Speaking of the alleged proffered kingdom at the first advent, Chafer says: "It was a bona fide offer, and, had they received him as their King, the nation's hopes would have been realized" (*The Kingdom in History and Prophecy,* p. 56).

To resort to hyperliteralism when reading what the Bible has to say about the kingdom of God is to court . resulting beliefs such as those we have quoted. When one takes the spirit of these passages, however, letting them say only what God inspired his writers to say — one runs into no such problem. The spirit of the figurative language found in some parts of the Bible causes one to recognize Christ's millennial kingdom as an ongoing reality with the triumphant Messiah as its Head. The *spirit* of these passages would never lead to failures being attributed to our Lord, or to his plans being frustrated by weak human beings.

Many clear passages from the New Testament speak of the kingdom in present terms. These passages naturally present a dilemma to those millennialists who teach that the kingdom — which they acknowledge is also the millennium — is yet to be established. Some try to get around these passages by asserting that there are two different kingdoms mentioned in the New Testament. They distinguish between the kingdom of God and the kingdom of heaven. This alleged distinction does not solve their problem, for both terms actually are used synonymously in the New Testament.

Our Lord spoke of a kingdom being present in John's day. Matthew records our Lord as referring to that kingdom as "the kingdom of heaven." Luke, who is obviously recording either the same message or a message on the same subject, says our Lord spoke of "the kingdom of God." There can be but one obvious explanation for these two inspired men using different words to record the same truth: the two words were used synonymously by Christ and his followers. Matthew no doubt used the term "heaven" instead of "God" out of deference for his Jewish listeners who refrained from using the word "God." Luke was writing primarily to Gentiles and thus had no such language problem.

"And from the days of John the Baptist until now *the kingdom of heaven* suffereth violence, and men of violence take it by force. For all the prophets and the law prophesied unto John" (Matt. 11:12, 13, italics added).

"The law and the prophets were until John: from that time the gospel of *the kingdom of God* is preached, and every man entereth violently into it" (Luke 16:16, italics added).

In these two passages let it be noted that the messenger spoken of in both instances is John. Let it be noted further that the message of John was said to begin where the law and the prophets left off. His message was about a kingdom. In one passage that kingdom is called the kingdom of *God,* while in the other it is called the kingdom of *heaven.* The time was the same, the man was the same, and the message was the same in both cases. Yet that message could be described by either of two names. Why? Because these two names were synonymous.

Our Lord's instructions upon sending out the twelve show conclusively that the terms "kingdom of heaven" and "kingdom of God" are synonymous in Scripture. "And as ye go, preach, saying, The kingdom of *heaven* is at hand" (Matt. 10:7, italics added). "And he sent them forth to preach the kingdom of *God,* and to heal the sick" (Luke 9:2, italics added). Here again these two inspired writers are describing a single event; yet each man uses a different synonym.

It is said of our Lord that he preached the kingdom of *heaven,* and also that he preached the kingdom of *God* (compare Matt. 4:17 with Mark 1:14, 15). Certainly our Lord did not preach two conflicting messages at the same time.

Indeed, the Lord used these two terms synonymously in one statement. "And Jesus said unto his disciples, Verily I say unto you, It is hard for a rich man to enter *the kingdom of heaven.* And again I say unto you, it is easier for a camel to go through a needle's eye, than for a rich man to enter into *the kingdom of God"* (Matt. 19:23, 24, italics added). Here we see a case of Hebrew parallelism in which the speaker says the same thing twice, for effect.

These scriptures show conclusively that the kingdom of heaven and the kingdom of God are one and the same. Therefore, dispensationalists are looking for a future millennial kingdom which in reality has been in existence since the first advent of our Lord. They admit that *whenever* the Davidic kingdom is set up on the earth Israel's hope will have been realized. They also admit that one kingdom of heaven came into existence with the birth of the Christian church. They further admit that the kingdom of God is the millennium.

This forms a syllogism, based on the dispensationalist's own admission that the kingdom of God and the millennium are one and the same. (1) Whenever the kingdom of God comes into existence, the millennium will also be in existence. (2) The kingdom of God is now in existence. (3) Therefore, the millennium is now in existence.

The millennial kingdom, which John describes in symbolic language, is a complete period of time during which Christ reigns in

70

the hearts of his people. This period began at the crucifixion (where Christ overcame Satan in fulfillment of Genesis 3:15) and will end at the second advent.

### Tribulation

Amillenarians believe the church age is marked out for almost constant tribulation. This tribulation (persecution) began when Satan was defeated at the cross. The twelfth chapter of Revelation relates how Satan tried to defeat Christ, and how that, failing in this, he turned his wrath upon the bride of Christ. This tribulation will grow progressively worse, culminating in the appearing of the anti-christ just preceding the second advent of Christ.

Will the church go through "the great tribulation"? Reams have been written on this question. Some denominations have suffered splits over the question — breaking up into pretribulation rapturists, posttribulation rapturists, and midtribulation rapturists. One of these groups argues that the church will be raptured *before* (pre) "the great tribulation"; another group says the church will not be raptured until *after* (post) "the great tribulation"; and yet a third group claims the church will be raptured half way through (mid) "the great tribulation."

Before this argument can be settled we must have a definition of terms. What is meant by "the great tribulation"? This term is taken from Matthew 24:21, where the Lord said: ". . . for then shall be great tribulation, such as hath not been from the beginning of the world until now, no, nor ever shall be." Our Lord is speaking of what he termed earlier (verse 15) "the abomination of desolation, which was spoken of through Daniel the prophet."

And what was the abomination of desolation spoken of by Daniel the prophet? The answer to this question lies in a comparison of parallel verses. "But when ye see Jerusalem compassed with armies, then know that her desolation is at hand" (Luke 21:20). One will want to study the verses immediately following this one, as well as the verses immediately following Matthew 21:24 in order to see that these are two verses on the same subject. In both passages Jesus predicts the abomination and immediately warns his listeners that when this event comes they should flee to the mountains, etc.

71

Actually, then, these theologians are haggling over whether or not the church will, in the future, go through something which already has happened! The church has already gone through the great tribulation. This took place in A.D. 70 when Titus, the Roman general, led his armies in the destruction of Jerusalem. God did not rapture his church before, or even midway through, the great tribulation. He protected her *through* it, just as he had promised to do in every time of testing. While approximately one and one half million non-believing Jews were killed by the armies of Titus during the Jewish Wars, all believing Christians (Jew and Gentile) fled to Pella, fifty miles away, and escaped harm. In this they were acting on the words of Christ that they should flee to the mountains when they saw the abomination of desolation coming upon Jerusalem, i.e., when they saw the armies surrounding the city (compare Matt. 24: 15,16 with Luke 21:20,21).

Although this particular tribulation is history, one still wonders how any serious student of the Bible could be surprised by the church going through tribulation. God nowhere promised to take the church out of the way of persecution. He promised, rather, to make her triumphant in the midst of persecution. Read John 17:15.

The tribulation referred to above — being that recorded in Matthew 24:15, Mark 13:14, and Luke 21:20 — was primarily of a physical nature and was visited upon Israel as a nation. The church suffers tribulation which is primarly spiritual. "For we wrestle not against flesh and blood, but against principalities, against the powers, against the world-rulers of this darkness, against the spiritual hosts of wickedness in the heavenly places" (Eph. 6:12).

Some students of the Bible believe that the great tribulation spoken of by our Lord in Matthew 24:21 began in A.D. 70 under Titus, but that it actually continues until the end of history. This belief is based upon the statement of our Lord that, *"immediately after the tribulation of those days,"* his second coming would take place (Matt. 24:29, 30). There is much merit in this thought, since the second coming has not taken place, and since it would be difficult to construe "immediately" as meaning two or three thousand years after the event. The parallel passages make it clear, however, that our Lord spoke *primarily of* A.D. 70.

Will the church suffer persecution, i.e., go through tribulation? What saith the scripture? That the new-covenant Israel was to be bathed in persecution (tribulation) there can be no doubt as one reads the Bible. Not only was tribulation foretold in the New Testament, it was also looked upon as the badge of a genuine believer. Paul recounted his own hardships as a member of the church, then warned that ". . . all that would live godly in Christ Jesus shall suffer persecution" (II Tim. 3:12). That persecution is the lot of every Christian is evident from such passages as Revelation 7 where John describes every believer in heaven as one who came out of (through) great tribulation.

Contrary to popular opinion, it was not the 144,000 who came out of great tribulation there in Revelation 7. John had finished talking of the twelve tribes in verse 8. Then verse 9 takes up with the words, "After these things I saw, and behold, a great multitude, which no man could number, out of every nation and of all tribes and peoples and tongues, standing before the throne and before the Lamb, arrayed in white robes, and palms in their hands. . ." (Rev. 7:9). In verse 14 the elder is referring to verse 9 when he says to John: "These [the great multitude which no man could number, of verse 9] are they that come out of the great tribulation, and they washed their robes, and made them white in the blood of the Lamb. Therefore they are before the throne of God: and they serve him day and night. . ." (Rev. 7:14,15).

We see, then, that every believer, i.e., every member of the church, will have gone through great tribulation by the time he reaches heaven. Even a cursory glance at the book of Revelation, and other scriptures, will make it evident that "those who have washed their robes in the blood of the Lamb" is a description of every believer; this is why John saw them as a great multitude which could not be numbered.

John the Revelator's manner of introducing himself to his readers takes for granted the fact that tribulation is the lot of the church during the present kingdom age. "I John, your brother and partaker with you in the tribulation and kingdom and patience which are in Jesus, was in the isle that is called Patmos, for the word of God and the testimony of Jesus." John said that in Jesus one would find *tribulation,* a *kingdom,* and *patience* to endure the tribulations of that kingdom.

Jesus, our Lord, suffered from the moment he began his ministry. In fact, even as a child he was so threatened that it became necessary for his parents to flee with him to Egypt. Our Lord taught his disciples that all who follow him should be prepared to accept the ridicule and persecution of the world. Indeed, the first requirement of a genuine Christian is that he shoulder a cross. *The cross is the emblem of Christianity and symbolizes a struggle to the death between the forces of good and the forces of evil.*

"A disciple is not above his teacher, nor a servant above his Lord. It is enough for the disciple that he be as his teacher, and the servant as his Lord. If they called the master of the house Beelzebub, how much more them of his household!" (Matt. 10:24, 25).

"So that we ourselves glory in you in the churches of God for your patience and faith in all your persecutions and in the afflictions which ye endure; which is a manifest token of the righteous judgment of God; to the end that ye may be counted worthy of the kingdom of God, for which ye also suffer" (II Thess. 1:4,5).

"The kingdom of heaven is likened unto a certain king . . . and the rest laid hold on his servants and treated them shamefully, and killed them. . ." (Matt. 22:1-5).

"Beloved, think it not strange concerning the fiery trial among you, which cometh upon you to prove you, as though a strange thing happened unto you: but insomuch as ye are partakers of Christ's suffering, rejoice; that at the revelation of his glory also ye may rejoice with exceeding joy. If ye are reproached for the name of Christ, blessed are ye; because the Spirit of glory and the Spirit of God resteth upon you. For let none of you suffer as a murderer, or a thief, or an evil-doer, or as a meddler in other men's matters: but if a man suffer as a Christian, let him not be ashamed; but let him glorify God in this name. For the time is come for judgment to begin at the house of God: and if it begin first at us, what shall be the end of them that obey not the gospel of God? And if the righteous is scarcely saved, where shall the ungodly and sinner appear? Wherefore let them also that suffer according to the will of God commit their souls in well-doing unto a faithful Creator" (I Peter 4:12-19).

74

"If the world hateth you, ye know that it hath hated me before it hated you. If ye were of the world, the world would love its own: but because ye are not of the world, but I chose you out of the world, therefore the world hateth you. Remember the word that I said unto you, a servant is not greater than his lord. If they persecuted me, they will also persecute you; if they kept my word, they will keep yours also" (John 15:18-20).

The Scriptures show conclusively that tribulation is a natural by-product of genuine Christianity. This was prophesied in the Old Testament, announced by the forerunner of Christ, attested to by the Lord himself, taught by his disciples, and has been experienced by every true follower of Christ.

Although the church suffers severe persecution, it nonetheless reigns triumphantly with Christ. The Christian is a pilgrim in this land of persecution; his true home is in heaven. "For our citizenship is in heaven; whence also we wait for a Saviour, the Lord Jesus Christ: who shall fashion anew the body of our humiliation, that it may be conformed to the body of his glory, according to the working whereby he is able even to subject all things unto himself" (Phil. 3:20,21).

"These things have I spoken unto you, that in me ye may have peace. In the world ye have tribulation: but be of good cheer; I have overcome the world" (John 16:33).

The tribulation of the church began with the first advent of our Lord as he entered the arena to fight Satan in his own territory (Matt. 12:29). Our Lord's persecution was climaxed at Calvary. Now Satan has turned his fierce wrath upon the church. The church already has witnessed many persecutions. However, these persecutions will grow progressively worse until finally they culminate in the appearance of the antichrist himself.


*Satan Shall Be Loosed for a Short Time*

The last persecutor of the church will be the antichrist himself. We know from such scriptures as II Thessalonians 2 that the antichrist will be on the earth at the time of the second advent, and that only the second coming of Christ will bring persecution to its end. We believe this tribulation under the antichrist, whom Paul calls the

75

man of sin or the lawless one, is to take place while Satan is loosed for his little season. In other words, we take II Thessalonians 2:8 and Revelation 20:3b (dealing with the loosing of Satan) to be parallel passages — speaking of one and the same event.

John taught that many antichrists already were in the world at the time of his writing (I John 2:18). This substantiates our position that the church will always be going through tribulation. And the scriptural teaching that these lesser demons will some day be succeeded by the main antichrist (Satan himself) bears out the amillennial teaching that the present on-going persecution against the church will grow progressively worse until the second coming of Christ ushers in the eternal state which alone will be a period free from persecution.

Satan is a great imitator. God has his holy angels, Satan has his angels; God places his mark upon his people (Rev. 7:3), Satan also marks his followers (Rev. 13:16); God rewards obedience with life, Satan also rewards his followers for their obedience to him ("the wages of sin is death"); even in the arrangement of his forces Satan imitates God. For on the one hand we have God, angels, Christians; on the other hand we have Satan, demons, wicked followers.

Satan will be an imitator to the end. Since Christ has predicted his second advent, Satan too must have a counterpart. In II Thessalonians 2 Paul teaches that antichrist will be "revealed" (vss. 6-8), and speaks, in verse 9, of the "coming" of antichrist. As Christ will appear the second time as God incarnate, the antichrist will appear (imitating the second advent) as Satan incarnate. Here we have the real significance of the word "antichrist." According to Greek lexicons "anti" not only means to oppose Christ, it also means "for, instead of" Christ (the anointed One). When antichrist comes he will claim that he is the Messiah and that this is his (Messiah's) second advent. He will oppose Christ while acting *as* Christ.

The little season during which the lawless one is loosed would seem to be a time of testing and refining for God's people. It will be a time which separates the mere professors from the genuine believers. Though many will have a form of godliness, one who stands for the true faith will be greatly persecuted.

Lawlessness is portrayed as being perhaps the outstanding characteristic of the "little time" during which antichrist is loosed. An interesting comparison may be made between the description in

76

II Thessalonians 2 and that in Revelation 20. Paul refers to antichrist as "the lawless one," while John says that Satan will be "loosed for a little time" (Rev. 20:3). In both these word pictures one gains the impression of unrestrained disregard for law and authority. Since God is the author of law and order, this looseness or lawlessness is in direct opposition to the known will of God. This is antichrist's ultimate aim, i.e., to exalt himself above God (II Thess. 2:40).

One thought relating to the antichrist usually is overlooked. Scripture nowhere states that he will be recognized for what he is. Rather, he will appear much as did the serpent in Eden — cunning and deceiving. He will appear as a religious leader!

In view of the present circumstances, antichrist might well be already on the scene. The ecumenical movement is made to order for one person (antichrist) to assume the leadership of an apostate super "church." This person could well be the Pope of Rome. Leading ecumenists are bowing more and more in that direction. The last decade has witnessed a Romish flavor of ritualism in many major denominations. Many altar-centered churches were, until recently, Bible-centered. If antichrist has not been the architect in Protestantism in recent years he could scarcely find a more opportune atmosphere in which to launch his program!

The New Testament teaches that certain things are to precede the second advent. Among these are apostasy, self-love, persecution, and the antichrist. That the first three of these abound today seems self-evident. We have indicated our suspicion that antichrist has already appeared and is leading a spiritual warfare against the kingdom of God.

We believe the Bible teaches that this warfare between Christ and Satan began at the birth of Christ, that it has reached climaxes at certain points in history — examples are the destruction of Jerusalem in A.D. 70, the fall of Rome in A.D. 476, the Inquisitions, and so forth — and that it will end with Satan himself personified as the antichrist. When antichrist has taken personal leadership of all satanic forces, and when it looks as if he will actually overcome the Christian church, then the trumpet will sound and Christ will appear.

That antichrist will be persecuting the church when Christ appears is learned from such scriptures as the following.

"It is a righteous thing with God to recompense affliction to them that afflict you, and to you that are afflicted rest with us, at the revelation of the Lord Jesus from heaven with the angels of his power in flaming fire, rendering vengeance to them that know not God. . ." (II Thess. 1:6-8).

". . . touching the coming of our Lord Jesus Christ, and our gathering together unto him . . . it will not come, except the falling away come first, and the man of sin be revealed, the son of perdition, he that opposeth and exalteth himself against all that is called God or that is worshipped; so that he sitteth in the temple of God, setting himself forth as God . . . and then shall be revealed the lawless one, whom the Lord Jesus shall slay with the breath of his mouth, and bring to nought by the manifestation of his coming" (II Thess. 2:1-8).

"And when the thousand years are finished, Satan shall be loosed out of his prison, and shall come forth to deceive the nations which are in the four corners of the earth, Gog and Magog, to gather them together to war: the number of whom is as the sand of the sea. And they went up over the breadth of the earth, and compassed the camp of the saints about, and the beloved city: and fire came down out of heaven, and devoured them. And the devil that deceived them was cast into the lake of fire and brimstone, where are also the beast and the false prophet: and they shall be tormented day and night for ever and ever" (Rev. 20:7-15).

In these passages Paul and John speak of the same event. Both speak of a persecution of the church immediately preceding the second advent, both refer to the persecutor and to his final end. And both refer, poetically, to the second coming of Christ as "fire from heaven."

This great and final battle between God's forces and those of Satan will signal the second coming of Christ to earth, since his coming will put down the antichrist and bring final victory to the church, the Israel of God (II Thess. 2:8).

"And at that time shall Michael stand up, the great prince who standeth for the children of thy people; and there shall be a time of trouble, such as never was since there was a nation even to that time: and at that time thy people shall be delivered, every one that shall be found written in the book. And many of them that sleep in the dust of the earth shall awake, some to everlasting life, and some to shame and everlasting contempt" (Dan. 12:1,2).

". . . for it |the second coming| will not be, except the falling away come first, and the man of sin be revealed, the son of perdition, he that opposeth and exalteth himself against all that is called God or that is worshipped; so that he sitteth in the temple of God, setting himself forth as God. . . . For the mystery of lawlessness doth already work: only there is one that restraineth now, until he be taken out of the way. And then shall be revealed the lawless one, whom the Lord Jesus shall slay with the breath of his mouth, and bring to nought by the manifestation of his coming; even he, whose coming is according to the working of Satan with all power and signs and lying wonders, and with all deceit of unrighteousness for them that perish; because they received not the love of the truth, that they might be saved. And for this cause God sendeth them a working of error, that they should believe a lie: that they all might be judged who believed not the truth, but had pleasure in unrighteousness" (II Thess. 2:1-12).

"And I saw another sign in heaven, great and marvellous, seven angels having seven plagues, which are the last, *for in them is finished the wrath of God*" (Rev. 15:1, italics added).

"And men were scorched with great heat: and they blasphemed the name of God who hath the power over these plagues; and they repented not to give him glory. And the fifth angel poured out his bowl upon the throne of the beast; and his kingdom was darkened; and they gnawed their tongues for pain, and they blasphemed the God of heaven because of their pains and their sores; and they repented not of their works. And the sixth poured out his bowl upon the great river, the river Euphrates; and the water thereof was dried up, that the way might be made ready for the kings that come from the sunrising. And I saw coming out of the mouth of the dragon, and out of the mouth of the beast, and out of the mouth of the false prophet, three unclean spirits, as it were frogs: for they are spirits of demons, working signs; which go forth unto the kings of the whole world, to gather them together unto the war of the great day of God, the Almighty. (Behold, I come as a thief. Blessed is he that watcheth, and keepeth his garments, lest he walk naked, and they see his shame.) And they gathered them together into the place which is called in Hebrew Har-Mageddon. And the seventh poured out his bowl upon the air; and there came forth a great voice out of the temple, from the throne, saying, It is done; and there were lightnings, and voices, and thunders: and there was a great earthquake, such as was not since there were men upon the earth, so great an earthquake, so mighty. And the great city was divided into three parts, and the cities of the nations fell: and Babylon the great was remembered in the sight of God, to give unto her the cup of the wine of the fierceness of his wrath. And every island fled away, and the mountains were not found. And great hail, every stone about the weight of a talent, cometh down out of heaven upon men: and men blasphemed God because of the plague of the hail; for the plague thereof is exceeding great" (Rev. 16:9-21).

"And when the thousand years are finished, Satan shall be loosed out of his prison, and shall come forth to deceive the nations which are in the four corners of the earth, Gog and Magog, to gather them together to the war: the number of whom is as the sand of the sea. And they went up over the breadth of the earth, and compassed the camp of the saints about, and the beloved city: and fire came down out of heaven, and devoured them. And the devil that deceived them was cast into the lake of fire and brimstone, where are also the beast and the false prophet; and they shall be tormented day and night for ever and ever" (Rev. 20:7-10).

When these scriptures are collated, they teach the following:

1. The wicked will suffer tribulation as well as the righteous.

2. The wicked will not repent during this time of spiritual warfare.

3. Tribulation was already going on in Paul's day, but Paul predicted a worse time when the antichrist would be released.

4. During the time of tribulation, the wicked, led by antichrist himself, will oppose the righteous.

5. The time of this warfare — this time of increased tribulation — is to be one of the last historical events to take place in this present world.

6. The coming of Christ will put down the antichrist, thereby ending all tribulation for the saints.

7. It is nowhere stated that Christians will recognize the antichrist when he appears. This being so, we may well be going through the "little time" already. Current events certainly favor such a conclusion.

80

John says antichrists are those who deny that Jesus is the Christ. This, according to John, is to deny God the Father. We have said that antichrists of John's day were henchmen or demons of the main antichrist who was yet to come. When he comes he will not be satisfied merely to deny the Christ; he will represent himself as being the Christ.

Antichrist imitates just about every act of Christ's. Both had a first 'advent into the world. Both have angels serving them. Both have missionaries. Each will reward his followers: "For the wages of sin is death; but the free gift of God is eternal life in Christ Jesus our Lord" (Rom. 6:23). And, since the Lord is destined to return a second time to the earth, Satan too is planning a second appearance, in the form of the antichrist. In every case he imitates the Christ.

Antichrist's stay on the earth will be short-lived, as God counts time. There is not a shadow of doubt as to which side will win the battle of Armageddon. Although Satan will even appear to overcome the church, and will be at his height of persecuting the righteous when Christ appears, that appearing will put Satan down with finality. He will then be cast into the lake of fire, where he will remain to suffer throughout eternity (Rev. 20:10).

Since it looks as though antichrist may already be abroad in the land, every genuine believer should rest heavily on the promises of God, and count it a joy to suffer for the cause of Christ. This suffering, says Paul, could not even be compared with the blessings awaiting God's people at the second coming.

# VII

## THE SECOND ADVENT

Our generation has witnessed many marvelous things. More physical and scientific advancements have been made in the last half century than were made in the preceding two thousand years. Since the turn of the century man has split the atom, broken the sound barrier, perfected many disease cures, plumbed the depth of the seas, and orbited the earth, to name but a few of his accomplishments.

However, the most stupendous phenomenon ever witnessed is yet future. It is definitely fixed on God's agenda, and the exact time is known only to him. We speak of the second coming of Christ to the earth. Let the reader envision a day when routine activities go on as usual (read Matt. 24:37-39). People are buying, selling, working, resting, sinning, worshiping — when suddenly a sound is heard from heaven like that of a trumpet. Every gaze will be drawn heavenward (Rev. 1:7) to see Jesus Christ — attended by a heavenly host — descending upon a cloud.

According to the Scriptures, the second advent is to be literal, bodily, visible. This statement is based upon such scriptures as the following.

". . . as they were looking, he was taken up; and a cloud received him out of their sight. And while they were looking stedfastly into heaven as he went, behold, two men stood by them in white apparel; who also said, Ye men of Galilee, why stand ye looking into heaven? this Jesus, who was received up from you into heaven, shall so come in like manner as ye beheld him going into heaven" (Acts 1:9-12).

"For the Lord himself shall descend from heaven, with a shout, with the voice of the archangel, and with the trump of God. . ." (I Thess. 4:16).

The angels taught that Jesus — the same Jesus whom they watched go, in a bodily form, into heaven — would come again

82

to the earth *in like manner*. And Paul was emphatic in saying the Lord *himself* shall descend from heaven.

### Defining Our Terms

Not every mention of a "coming" or "appearing" of our Lord refers to the second advent. Confusing doctrines have grown out of the attempt of some to apply too many scriptures to the second coming of Christ. Let us take as an example the words of Jesus recorded in Matthew 10:23: ". . . ye shall not have gone through the cities of Israel, till the Son of man be come." Although many have used this verse to prove a point with reference to the second coming, actually it has no reference to it at all. The Lord was sending out the twelve on an earthly mission, and promised them that he would personally join them before they finished the assignment.

Another example of misapplication of Scripture on this doctrine would be our Lord's prediction of his transfiguration. In Matthew 16:28 we find these words: "Verily I say unto you, there are some of them that stand here, who shall in no wise taste of death, till they see the Son of man coming in his kingdom." Although many apply this prediction to the second advent, the verses which follow immediately after give the true fulfillment of the prophecy. For Matthew goes on to say that "after six days Jesus . . . was transfigured before them. . ." (Matt. 17:1,2).

In Matthew 24, our Lord very definitely speaks on two different subjects — the destruction of Jerusalem, which took place in A.D. 70, and the end of the world. Some make the mistake of applying this entire chapter to the second coming. It is only natural that these folk end up with conflicting doctrines.

### Synonymous Terms

The Greek language portrays two distinct types of action. One is linear action and could be illustrated by a line drawn by a pencil. The other is called punctilliar action, and this is illustrated by a single dot made by pressing the pencil lead against a sheet of paper. The second advent is to be a punctilliar type action, i.e., a single event, rather than something coming in different stages.

Throughout the New Testament many terms are used to describe the second coming of Christ. Such terms are used as, "the day of the Lord" (Acts 2:20; II Thess. 2:2; II Peter 3:10), "the day of the Lord Jesus" (I Cor. 5:5; II Cor. 1:14), "the day of our Lord Jesus Christ" (I Cor. 1:8), "the day of Jesus Christ" (Phil. 1:6), "the day of Christ" (Phil. 1:10; 2:16), "the day of God" (II Peter 3:12; Rev. 16:14), "that day" (Matt. 7:22; 24:36; 26:29; Luke 10:12; II Thess. 1:10; II Tim. 1:18), "the last day" (John 6:39, 40, 44, 54; 11:24; 12:48) "his day" (Luke 17:24), "the revelation of Christ" (II Thess. 1:7; I Peter 1:7, etc.), "the appearing of Christ" (I Tim. 6:14; II Tim. 4:1,8), "the coming of Christ" (I Cor. 15:23; I Thess. 2:19; James 5:7).

Since each "day" quoted above refers to the same event, the terms relating to the second advent actually may be reduced to four — appearing, revelation, coming, and day.

Dispensationalists attempt to make these four terms refer to many separate steps or stages in the second coming of Christ, with a lapse of time and other events separating each step. However, one need not even have a knowledge of Greek in order to disprove this claim. For the lexicons and Bible dictionaries generally agree that these terms have the following meanings.

*Parousia:* "arrival," "presence." This word is translated "coming" in the New Testament. The parousia (of Christ) occurs in the following passages: I Cor. 15:23; I Thess. 2:19; 3:13; 4:15; 5:23; II Thess. 2:1, 8.

"The word expresses two closely connected ideas of arrival and presence. *Parousia* signifies 'becoming present' and 'being present.' Somewhat of an analogy would be our English word 'visit,' " (Geerhardus Vos, *The Pauline Eschatology*, p. 74).

*Epiphanias:* "appearing," "a manifestation," "brightness." This is from a root word meaning to "shine upon," "give light," "become visible."

*Apokalupto:* "disclosure," "appearing," "coming," "lighten," "manifestation," "be revealed," "revelation." This is from a root word meaning to "take the cover off," i.e., "disclose," "reveal."

84

*Hemera:* "day." "fig. a period (always defined more or less clearly by the context)" (*Greek Dictionary of the New Testament.* p. 35; James Strong, *The Exhaustive Concordance of the Bible*).

One can readily see that these four terms — coming, appearing, revelation, day — portray synonymous concepts, and that they refer to a singular event. These different terms are used, not to depict different occasions, but rather to draw attention to unique aspects of that one great occasion. Each is simply a different facet of a single gem. In one context the inspired writer intended to emphasize the certainty of Jesus' *coming;* another writer wished to elucidate the fact that our Lord's majesty — which is presently hidden from view — will be *revealed* at his second coming; another text will bring comfort to the believer as he is reminded that our Lord will some day be bodily *present* and that his appearing will be visible for all to behold.

This is no different from the four accounts of the life of our Lord recorded in the four Gospels. Certainly no one would suggest that the Gospels record four different lives of Christ, each taking place at a different time in history. Still there are four different emphases there; one writer brings out the kingship of Christ, another his manhood, another his miracles, and yet another his eternality. Here again are four sides of one personality, four facets of one great jewel. And so it is with the different aspects of the one second coming of Christ to the earth. It is to be multi-dimensional and each term simply views it from one certain angle. Dr. Harold Ockenga says, "No exegetical justification exists for the arbitrary separation of the Coming of Christ and the Day of the Lord" (quoted from Norman F. Douty, *Has Christ's Return Two Stages?* p. 75).

A careful analysis of the following scriptures will make it self-evident that different terms used with reference to the second coming of Christ actually refer to a single event.

"And the Lord make you to increase and abound in love one toward another, and toward all men, even as we also do toward you; to the end he may establish your hearts unblameable in holiness before our God and Father *at the coming of our Lord Jesus with all his saints*" (I Tim. 6:14, italics added).

". . . waiting for the revelation of our Lord Jesus Christ" (I Cor. 1:7).

". . . that ye may be sincere and void of offense unto the day of Christ" (Phil. 1:10).

"Be patient therefore, brethren, until the coming of our Lord" (James 5:7).

". . . we should live soberly and righteously and godly in this present world; *looking for the blessed hope and appearing of the glory of the great God and our Saviour Jesus Christ*" (Titus 2:12,13, italics added).

Both Paul and James presuppose that some Christians will remain on the earth until Jesus' appearing. This can only mean that all these terms refer to one and the same event. The dispensationalists, on the other hand, contend that these terms refer to distinct and separate events and that only some of them will involve Christians while some will involve only the unrighteous.

### Day Versus Days

Much confusion has grown from the erroneous teaching that the last day and the last days are synonymous. Actually, each of these terms has a meaning distinct from the other. One refers to a duration of time covering a number of happenings, while the other refers to a single event.

In defining our terms, we gave Dr. Strong's definition of "day" as it is used in the New Testament. Dr. Strong correctly points out that the length of time involved in the period denoted by the word "day" is always defined for us by the context itself. With this thought before us, we wish to point out that the word "day," wherever it refers to the second coming, is always in the singular (punctilliar) vein. An extended period of time, when referred to in the New Testament, is always distinguished by the plural, i.e., *days* as distinguished from *day*. The reader is never left in doubt as to whether any given passage has reference to an extended period (linear action) or a given point in time (punctilliar action).

### In These Last Days

The New Testament makes clear the fact that the birth of Christ ushered in the last days (plural). This has been true at least since

86

the Day of Pentecost, for at that time the apostle Peter made the following statement.

". . . this is that which hath been spoken through the prophet Joel: And it shall be *in the last days,* saith God, I will pour forth of my Spirit upon all flesh: and your sons and your daughters shall prophesy, and your young men shall see visions, and your old men shall dream dreams: Yea and on my servants and on my hand-maidens *in those days* will I pour forth of my Spirit; and they shall prophesy. And I will show wonders in the heaven above, and signs on the earth beneath; blood, and fire, and vapor of smoke: The sun shall be turned into darkness, and the moon into blood, before the day of the Lord come, that great and notable day: And it shall be that whosoever shall call on the name of the Lord shall be saved" (Acts 2:16-21 — Peter quoted from Joel 2:28-32, italics added).

Peter said that those people on the Day of Pentecost witnessed events that had been predicted by the prophet Joel to happen in the last days. The fact that they happened was ample proof that the predicted time and events were present. So that the *last days* began with the first advent of our Lord and we are still in them.

The writer of Hebrews also informs us that the last days have already begun. Note the past tense in the following verses.

"God, having of old time spoken unto the fathers in the prophets by divers portions and in divers manners, hath *at the end of these* days spoken unto us in his Son, . . ." (Heb. 1:1,2, italics added).

". . . but now once at the end of the ages hath he been mani-fested to put away sin by the sacrifice of himself" (Heb. 10:26).

This is a clear reference to Christ and states that God has spoken directly through Jesus to the world. Only one event corresponds to a time when God spoke directly through a Son, and that event was the earthly ministry of our Lord. Therefore, the last days be-gan with the first advent.

In Paul's writings it is not difficult to see that the great apostle to the Gentiles taught that the people of his generation were already living in the eleventh hour of time.

"Now these things happened unto them by way of example; and they were written for our admonition upon whom the ends of the ages are come" (I Cor. 10:11).

The apostle Peter places the first advent of our Lord in the end of time as evidenced by his statement in I Peter 1:20. "Who was foreknown indeed before the foundation of the world, but *was* manifested at the end of the times for your sake, . . ." (italics added).

John is specific in saying, "Little children, it is the last hour" (I John 2:18).

Since we have seen that the Bible clearly teaches that we are in the last days, then it is a wresting of the Scriptures to picture the last days as being altogether future. And, since we are already in the last days, it follows that any event predicted for that period is either history, or else is in the process of being fulfilled during our present age.

When the New Testament speaks of then current or past periods, these are always in the plural. It speaks of the days of Herod (Matt. 2:1), the days of John the Baptist (Matt. 3:1; 11:12), the days of the prophets (Luke 4:25; Matt. 23:30), the days of tribulation (Matt. 24:19-22, 29), the days of Noah (Matt. 24:37), the days of Jesus' earthly ministry (Mark 1:9; Heb. 5:7). All these persons mentioned did certain things on a given day (singular), but the *periods* of their ministries are always in the plural (days).

### The Coming Last Day

The last day (singular), on the other hand, is still future, according to the teachings of the New Testament. In the New Testament one never reads, with reference to the second coming, of the days of judgment, the days of the Lord, the days of Jesus Christ, the days of the resurrection, the revelations, the comings, the appearings, or the like. This event is always spoken of in the singular — the day, the judgment, the resurrection, the coming.

"Many will say to me in that day, Lord, Lord, did we not prophesy by thy name. . ." (Matt. 7:22).

"Verily I say unto you, It shall be more tolerable for the land of Sodom and Gomorrah in the day of judgment, than for that city" (Matt. 10:15).

"For as the lightning, when it lighteneth out of the one part under the heaven, shineth unto the other part of heaven; so shall the Son of man be in his day" (Luke 17:24).

88

"After the same manner it shall be in the day that the Son of man is revealed. In that day, he that shall be on the housetop, and his goods in the house, let him not come down to take them away. . ." (Luke 17:30,31).

"And this is the will of him that sent me, that of all that which he hath given me I should lose nothing, but should raise it up at the last day" (John 6:39,40,44,54).

"Martha saith unto him, I know that he shall rise again in the resurrection at the last day" (John 11:24).

". . . the word that I speak, the same shall judge him in the last day" (John 12:48).

"The sun shall be turned into darkness and the moon into blood, before the day of the Lord come" (Acts 2:20).

"But after thy hardness and impenitent heart treasurest up for thyself wrath in the day of wrath and revelation of the righteous judgment of God" (Rom. 2:5).

These and many other scriptures point up the fact that the second coming will take place on a given day rather than be extended over more than one day. The second coming, in other words, will occur on the last day of these last days. We are already in these last days and ever drawing nearer to the last day.


### *The Two Terms — Day and Days — Used Together*

One can hardly fail to see the contrast in the New Testament use of day versus days. This contrast is pointed up even more sharply in passages wherein the words are used together. An example follows.

"And as it came to pass in the *days* of Noah, even so shall it be also in the *days* of the Son of man. They ate, they drank, they married, they were given in marriage, until the *day* that Noah entered into the ark, and the flood came, and destroyed them all. Likewise even as it came to pass in the *days* of Lot; they ate, they drank, they bought, they sold, they planted, they builded; but in the *day* that Lot went out from Sodom it rained fire and brimstone from heaven, and destroyed them all: after the same manner shall it be in the *day* the Son of man is revealed. In *that day*, he that shall be on the housetop, and his goods in the house, let him not go down to take them away: and let him that is in the field likewise not return back" (Luke 17:26-31, italics added).

Here Luke compares the ministry of our Lord with the ministries of Noah and Lot. He also likens the climax of the second coming with the climaxes of the other men. The entire period included in Noah's time on earth is referred to in the plural, i.e., "the *days* of Noah." Then, says Luke, on a certain day during Noah's days on earth, he entered the ark. Lot likewise on a certain day, during his days on earth, went out from Sodom and on that *day* an eventful thing happened. Then, using these well-known events as examples, Luke says that during the days of Christ things are just as they were during the days of Noah, i.e., people go on eating, drinking, getting married, being generally unconcerned about the things of God. Then, says Luke, there will come a day (singular) when people will be called to account. Luke speaks of three persons in history — Noah, Lot, Jesus — and in the case of each one he uses a plural ("in the days of") and a singular ("in the day," "in that day").

### Characteristics of the Second Coming

God has reserved some knowledge concerning the second coming to himself. For example, no man knows the time it will take place. Only God knows that (Matt. 24:36). However, the Bible does tell us many things concerning the second advent. We know, for example:

1. It will come suddenly (Rev. 22:29; Luke 17:24).

2. It will come unexpectedly (Matt. 24:39; Luke 12:40; I Thess. 5:2; Rev. 16:15).

3. It will be seen by all (Rev. 1:7).

4. It will be heard by all (Matt. 16:27; Mark 13:26; II Thess. 1:7).

5. It will be accompanied by angels and clouds (Matt. 16:27; 24:30,31; 25:31,32).

## Some Results of the Second Coming

1. It will complete the first advent (Heb. 9:28). Actually, the first and second advents of Christ complement each other. One is not complete without the other. Nor does this contradict our earlier statement that the second coming itself will not be in stages. The second coming is itself a complete and singular stage in God's plan.

Our Lord set eschatology in motion by his first advent into the world. He established the new covenant, and threw open the door of salvation to all peoples by tearing down the middle wall of partition existing between Jew and Gentile (Eph. 2:11-16). The first advent also manifested the kingdom, and began the judgment of the world. However, none of these will be consummated until the second coming.

2. Complete salvation will be realized. One of the best illustrations of the twofold nature of our salvation is found in Hebrews. "So Christ, also, having been once offered to bear the sins of many, shall appear a second time apart from sin, to them that wait for him, unto salvation" (Heb. 9:28).

Jesus came, in the fullness of time, and became the perfect sacrifice to purchase a perfect salvation for all who will believe in him. And each person who has accepted Christ as Savior has been saved eternally and can never be condemned with the world (John 4:14; 10:28; Rom. 5:1; 8:1). He has already been delivered from the wrath to come (I Thess. 1:10). Still there is a tension between what the believer is and what he is to become. Our immortal souls are still housed in mortal bodies which will remain mortal until our Lord returns a second time (Rom. 8:23).

Peter speaks of the different aspects of salvation. He points out that the resurrection of Christ assured believers an incorruptible inheritance. Yet he says that the complete enjoyment of this inheritance is reserved in heaven and that we are "guarded through faith unto a salvation ready to be revealed in the last time" (I Peter 1:3-5). So that the Christian has been saved, he is being saved, and he is waiting to be saved from the wrath to come. This is illustrated in passages such as Romans 5:9-11.

3. The second coming of Christ will bring about an eternal separation. Today there is intercourse between the living saved and living unsaved. When the Lord returns, the great gulf between

them will be eternally solidified. The standing of each person when the Lord returns will be his standing throughout eternity. The lost person — Jew and Gentile — will have sinned away his last opportunity. And the Christian will have had his last opportunity to witness to the lost with a view toward winning souls for Christ. The day of salvation will have ended, the door of mercy will have closed (Matt. 24:37-39). In drawing this comparison between the flood in Noah's day and the second coming, our Lord points up a lesson that is inescapable. ". . . Noah entered into the ark, and they knew not until the flood came, and took them all away; so shall be the coming of the Son of man" (Matt. 24:39).

We know — and the Lord here reminds his listeners of this fact — that, once the flood came, not another soul entered the ark. Jesus said, "So shall be the coming of the Son of man." We find this same analogy in Matthew 25:1-13, "And they that were ready went in with him. . . ." All others were turned away because the separation had been made final, once the bridegroom appeared — or once the door of the ark had been closed at the appearance of the flood waters.

"But when the Son of man shall come in his glory, and all the angels with him, then shall he sit on the throne of his glory: and before him shall be gathered all the nations: and he shall separate them one from another, as the shepherd separateth the sheep from the goats; and he shall set the sheep on the right hand, but the goats on the left. Then shall the King say unto them on his right hand, Come, ye blessed of my Father, inherit the kingdom prepared for you from the foundation of the world: . . . Then shall he say also unto them on the left hand, Depart from me, ye cursed, into the eternal fire which is prepared for the devil and his angels: . . . And these shall go away into eternal punishment: but the righteous into eternal life" (Matt. 25:31-46).

"So shall be the coming of the Son of man. Then shall two men be in the field; one is taken, and one is left; two women shall be grinding at the mill; one is taken, and one is left" (Matt. 24:39-41).

"Again, the kingdom of heaven is like unto a net, that was cast into the sea, and gathered of every kind: which, when it was filled, they drew up on the beach; and they sat down, and gathered the good into vessels, but the bad they cast away" (Matt. 13:47).

"So shall it be in the end of the world; the angels shall come forth, and sever the wicked from among the righteous, and shall cast them into the furnace of fire: there shall be the weeping and the gnashing of teeth" (Matt. 13:47-49).

"Let both grow together until the harvest: and in the time of the harvest I will say to the reapers, Gather up first the tares, and bind them in bundles to burn them; but gather the wheat into my barn . . . the harvest is the end of the world. . ." (Matt. 13:30-39).

When this separation takes place the saints will be rewarded and the wicked will be judged (II Thess. 1:10; Phil. 3:20,21; II Tim. 4:8; I Peter 1:13; 5:4; II Thess. 1:8).

4. The kingdom of God will be consummated. Jesus manifested the kingdom at his first coming. At the second advent it will be perfected, then turned over to God the Father by God the Son (I Cor. 15:24), so that God may be all in all. At this time the earth will be cleansed (Rom. 8:20,21; II Pet. 3:7), and evil elements will be removed and cast into hell. Then will God's will truly be done on earth as it is now done in heaven (I Cor. 15:24). Sin will then not exist outside of hell.

5. Another thing begun at the Lord's first advent, but to be completed or consummated at his second coming, is the defeat of Satan. The Scriptures clearly teach that Satan was defeated when Christ died on the cross. There the heel of the Savior bruised the head of the serpent in fulfillment of Genesis 3:15. However, Satan still goes around like a roaring lion seeking whom he may devour; and he would deceive even the elect *"if it were possible."* This is not possible, however, since the Savior bound Satan, i.e., limited his power so that he could no longer deceive the nations (Rev. 20:3). Satan, though defeated, still has not had his sentence executed. It has been pronounced but not yet executed. Even Satan himself knows full well that his time is short (Rev. 12:12). Satan acts now under a suspended sentence. When Christ comes again that sentence will be executed and Satan will be cast eternally into the lake of fire (II Thess. 2:8; Rev. 20:10).

6. The second coming will bring history to its close, thereby ushering in the final state. Although men divide time into two periods divided by the birth of Christ, actually, the New Testament knows but two ages — the present age and the age to come (Matt. 12:32; Mark 10:30; Luke 20:34,35).

In reference to this world, the New Testament mind looked on it as that which had existed from the creation (Matt. 25:34), and which would end at the second coming of Christ (Matt. 13:39). The New Testament looked on the birth of Christ as marking the end-time of this present world (Heb. 9:26, etc.). The coming world is not to be a millennium which shall end, but the eternal state which has no end.

### Progressive Doctrinal Development

Each doctrine referred to above shows a progressive development. This can be said of many, perhaps most, doctrines dealt with in the New Testament. First the blade, then the ear, next the full grain in the ear (Mark 4:28, 29). Just about any doctrine of the New Testament could be used to illustrate this biblical rule of growth.

Paul was alive in Christ and looked forward only to an eternity with his Lord. Yet Paul taught that we are saved in hope; and if we *had* a thing, Paul said, it would be incongruous to go on hoping for it (Rom. 8:24, 25). In these areas we are dealing with divine paradoxes; and we need to keep in mind that a paradox is not a contradiction but merely a seeming contradiction. Man cannot comprehend every law of God.

### Related Events

In both his Thessalonian epistles Paul shows the relationship of the second coming to the rewarding of the righteous as well as to the punishing of the wicked. In both these epistles, too, men have made unfortunate chapter divisions. In I Thessalonians parts of chapters 4 and 5 form a unit, while in II Thessalonians chapters 1 and 2 belong together.

Whenever Paul, the foremost Christian theologian of all time, was inspired to write, many thoughts crowded in upon his great mind. One gains the impression from his thirteen epistles that this learned man thought faster than his hand could write, or faster even than he could dictate. In the two sections we have just mentioned,

Paul (1) began dealing with the second coming of Christ; (2) brought in, parenthetically, some thoughts on Christian living, etc.; (3) then returned to his main subject of the second coming. Upon returning to the subject, Paul uses different terminology in dealing with the same event — thus showing that these are synonymous terms.

". . . we that are alive, that are left unto *the coming of the Lord* shall in no wise precede them that are fallen asleep. For the Lord himself shall descend from heaven, with a shout, with the voice of the archangel, and with *the trump of God:* and *the dead in Christ shall rise first;* then we that are alive, that are left, shall together with them be caught up in the clouds, to meet the Lord in the air: and so shall we ever be with the Lord. Wherefore comfort one another with these words.

"But concerning the times and the seasons, brethren, ye have no need that aught be written unto you. For yourselves know perfectly that *the day of the Lord so cometh as a thief in the night.* When they are saying, Peace and safety then *sudden destruction cometh upon them,* as travail upon a woman with child; and they shall in no wise escape. *But ye, brethren, are not in darkness, that that day should overtake you as a thief*" (I Thess. 4:15 - 5:4, italics added).

Upon studying the above passage, one learns — and we have italicized these points — the following:

1. The coming of the Lord and the trump of God both describe the same event, seeing that Paul used them interchangeably.

2. At the coming of Christ (at the trump of God), the Christian dead will be raised and, along with the Christians then living, will be raptured to meet the Lord in the air.

3. So far as the unsaved are concerned, Jesus will come like a thief in the night, i.e., when least expected.

4. "That day" (here used interchangeably with the "coming of the Lord" and "the trump of God") will not come as a surprise to the faithful.

5. At the coming of the Lord (the last trump, that day), the unsaved will be destroyed. Also at the coming of the Lord (the last trump, that day), Christians will be resurrected. This being so, then both groups will remain together until the second coming.

"And to you that are afflicted rest with us, *at the revelation of the Lord Jesus from heaven* with the angels of his power in flaming fire, *rendering vengeance to them that know not God,* and to them that obey not the gospel of our Lord Jesus: *who shall suffer punishment, even eternal destruction from the face of the Lord* and from the glory of his might, *when he shall come to be glorified in his saints, and to be marvelled at in all them that believed* (because our testimony unto you was believed) *in that day. . . .*

"Now we beseech you, brethren, *touching the coming of our Lord Jesus Christ, and our gathering together unto him;* to the end that ye be not quickly shaken from your mind, nor yet be troubled, either by spirit, or by word, or by epistle as from us, as that the day of the Lord is just at hand" (II Thess. 1:7-2:2, italics added).

Paul is obviously speaking here (using first one term then another) of a single event. His subject does not change during the course of these verses. In these verses he speaks of "the revelation of the Lord Jesus," "the coming," "the glorification of the saints," which is to take place "in that day," at "the rapture," and "the day of the Lord." These all are used here by the apostle as synonymous terms. Paul also points out, in this same passage, that the saints will be glorified at the same time the unsaved are punished. Those who know not God "shall suffer punishment, even eternal destruction from the face of the Lord . . . when [at the time] he shall come to be glorified in his saints . . . in that day."

In I Corinthians 1:7, 8, Paul uses "the revelation of our Lord Jesus Christ" and "the day of our Lord Jesus Christ" interchangeably.

In I John 2:28, the "manifestation" of Christ, and his "coming" are used as synonymous terms.

| | End of World | Manifestation | Appearing | Trump | Revelation | Coming | Day |
|---|---|---|---|---|---|---|---|
| Saints Resurrected | | I Peter 5:4; Col. 3:4. | | I Cor. 15:51, 52; I Thess. 4:15, 16. | I Peter 1:13. | I Cor. 15:23; I Thess. 4:15. | John 6:39, 40, 44, 54. |
| General Judgment | Matt. 13:40. | | II Tim. 4:1. | | | Matt. 16:27. | Acts 17:31; I John 4:17; II Peter 2:9; 3:7. |
| Saints Rewarded | Matt. 13:40, 43. | Col. 3:4; I John 2:28; 3:2. | II Tim. 4:8; Heb. 9:28. | I Thess. 4:15-17. | I Peter 1:13; II Thess. 1:7-10. | II Thess. 1:10; I John 2:25; I Thess. 3:13; 4:15-17. | |
| Wicked Punished | Matt. 13:49, 50. | II Thess. 2:8. | | | II Thess. 1:7-10. | II Thess. 1:10; 2:8. | II Thess. 1:10; Rom. 2:5; Matt. 7:22, 23; Jude 6. |
| Separation | Matt. 13:40-43; 47-50. | | | Matt. 24:30, 31. | Luke 17:29, 30, 34, 35. | Matt. 24:37, 40; 25:31-46; Mark 13:26, 27. | |
| General Resurrection | | | | | | | John 11:24. |

A study of this chart will reveal that these events all are to be fulfilled at approximately the same time. Certainly no scriptural justification may be found for allowing long intervals of time between these events.

The chart shows, too, that the second coming of Christ is to be one event, though it is called by different names. This can be proved from the fact that many of the terms listed — such as "coming," "appearing," "manifestation," etc., are quoted from the same verses of Scripture.

When Jesus returns, both the wicked and the righteous will still be living on the earth. Both will witness his second coming and both will be involved in it. A comparison of scripture with scripture makes this fact forceably clear.

Many events are to find their fulfillment at the second coming of Christ. Among these are:

1. The resurrection, rapture, judgment, and rewarding of the saints.

2. The resurrection, judgment, and punishment of the wicked.

3. The close of history and ushering in of the final state.

4. The consummation of and turning over of the kingdom to God the Father.

5. The final punishment of Satan.

Each of these events has already been set in motion by the first advent, death, burial, and resurrection of our Lord. Each, however, awaits final fulfillment at the second advent.

# VIII

## RESURRECTION

Here we come to another of the key doctrines of the Bible. The resurrection was at the center of the message of the early church. Paul, the apostle to the Gentiles, staked the validity of his entire ministry on the fact of the resurrection. Without it, he said, all would be in vain.

Two types of resurrection are dealt with in the New Testament, and both are stressed. There are both a spiritual resurrection and a bodily resurrection. The first of these is the new birth, while the second is to take place at the *parousia*. Every Christian has already experienced the first resurrection; this took place the moment he surrendered his heart completely to Christ as Savior and Lord. Until that time the person was dead. "Ye were dead through your trespasses and sins" (Eph. 2:1). Paul, the theologian *par excellence,* teaches in the same verse that those who once were dead have been made alive (resurrected, brought from the dead) through Christ: "And you did he make alive. . . ."

Paul elaborates upon this teaching in other passages, such as the following.

". . . even when we were dead through our trespasses, *made us alive* together with Christ (by grace have ye been saved), *and raised us up* with him, and made us sit with him in the heavenly places, in Christ Jesus" (Eph. 2:5, 6).

"And you, being dead through your trespasses and the uncircumcision of your flesh, you, I say, did he make alive together with him, having forgiven us all our trespasses" (Col. 2:13).

"If ye then were raised together with Christ, seek the things that are above, where Christ is, seated on the right hand of God" (Col. 3:1).

This apostolic teaching was concurred in by such outstanding church fathers as Origen and Augustine, and was the teaching of most

99

if not all of the Reformers.   John Calvin and Martin Luther preached it strongly.

In chapter 5 of John's Gospel our Lord speaks of two resurrections.   These are the only two types of resurrection ever mentioned
by Jesus.   We believe he covered the entire subject in these verses.
If this be so, then every mention of resurrection in the Bible must
harmonize with one of these two.   He spoke clearly and to the point.
Here, as in all Bible study, the obscure passages must be interpreted
by the clear ones.

Upon examining these two resurrections (John 5:24-29), one
sees their different characteristics.

1. One is present, the other is future.
2. One is spiritual, the other is physical.
3. One is restricted to believers, the other includes everyone.

"Verily, verily, I say unto you, He that heareth my word, and
believeth him that sent me, hath eternal life, and cometh not into
judgment, but *hath passed out of death into life"* (John 5:24).

Having made this general statement, Jesus went on to explain
this doctrine: "Verily, verily I say unto you, *the hour* cometh, and
*now is,* when the dead shall hear the voice of the Son of God; and
they that hear shall live" (John 5:25).

It would be difficult to imagine language plainer than this concerning what constitutes the first resurrection of the Christian.   Jesus
said that in that generation dead people would hear his voice
and thereby be caused to live (be resurrected).   His words, "The
hour . . . *now is.* . . ." could not refer to the future.   Therefore,
we must seek another meaning for these words.   The biblical answer
is given in passages such as Ephesians 2:1,5,6; and I John 3:14
where the new birth is spoken of as a resurrection from the dead.

As a result of the first resurrection, and his part in it, the believer has spiritual life (John 5:24); old things are passed away,
behold, all things have become new (II Cor. 5:17); he is now a
citizen of heaven (Phil. 3:20; Heb. 13:14); he has begun already
to reign with Christ (Eph. 2:6; Col. 1:13; Rev. 1:6); he has already
been delivered from the power of the second death (I Thess. 1:10;
Rev. 20:6).   All these blessings will reach fruition at the second
resurrection; however, each has already begun as a result of the believer's participation in the first resurrection, i.e., his becoming a joint-

heir with Christ (through the new birth) who himself is the First Resurrection (John 11:24; I Cor. 15:20).

We have said of the first resurrection that it is present, spiritual, and that it involves only believers. Let us examine verse 25: "Verily, verily, I say unto you, the hour is coming *and now is,* when the dead shall hear the voice of the Son of God: and they that hear shall live." Our Lord's words "and now is" let us know that he was speaking of an event to take place at the time he spoke. Further, our Lord said the hour "now is" when dead people were to hear his voice and that those who heard would live.

We are interested here in the spiritual resurrection, which we take to be the new birth. Since the fall of Adam and Eve, all are spiritually dead. God said to Adam: "In the day you eat thereof you shall surely die." Adam lived physically a few hundred years after eating the forbidden fruit. However, God's word was none the less true; Adam did die that same day. He died a spiritual death. He lost the image of God in which he had been created. Since Adam died spiritually — and since he was the federal head of mankind — every person who has reached the age of accountability has become spiritually dead. Jesus, through the cross, made possible a resurrection from this spiritual death. When he arose from the grave our Lord conquered death. Actually, then, our Lord himself is the First Resurrection. Let us reconcile this statement with our previous statement that the new birth is the first resurrection for the Christian. Before conversion every person is spiritually dead (compare Eph. 2:1,5,6 and I John 3:14). Paul teaches that the believer is partaker with Christ in the crucifixion and also in his resurrection (Rom. 6:6; Col. 3:3). Thus, to be born again is to have part in the first resurrection.

Commenting on scriptures such as Colossians 3:3,4 and Ephesians 2:6, Ridderbos makes an enlightening statement: "Here the mystical, spiritual interpretation is an utter failure. One must rather say that Paul, when applying to the Church not only the Cross and death of Christ but also His exaltation until the parousia, is thinking in Categories quite different from mystical ones. It is not true that Christ first died for those who are His, who only afterwards also die and rise with Him, spiritually, mystically or ethically. No, when He died on Golgotha, they also died with Him, and when He arose in the garden of Joseph of Arimathea, they were raised together with

101

Him. Paul actually says it himself in so many words in 2 Corinthians 5:14: 'We thus judge, that one died for all, therefore all died' (Col. 3:3), or 'We who died to sin, how shall we any longer live therein?' (Rom. 6:2); the apostle does not appeal to the conversion of the faithful, but to their being included in Christ's death. And the same holds true for the resurrection, the exaltation in heaven, the coming back of the Church with Christ. Whatever happened to Christ, happened to the Church, not only analogously or metaphorically, but in the historical sense of the word. She was included in Him, was, and is, present in Him throughout all the phases of the great history of salvation" (Herman N. Ridderbos, *When the Time Had Fully Come, Studies in New Testament Theology*, p. 55).

In this same sense, the Christian has already had part in the first resurrection. For Christ is the Resurrection (John 11:25); and since the first resurrection has happened to Christ, it has also happened to every genuine convert. Our resurrection, like our dying to sin, took place at our conversion — both being retroactive through the saving power of Christ. And — since every Christian is a joint-heir with Christ — the second death can have no more power over us than it can have over him. This statement must be made reverently; nevertheless, it is scripturally true.

Having spoken of the spiritual resurrection, our Lord went on to speak of a general physical resurrection.

"Marvel not at this [see vs. 25]: for the hour cometh in which all that are in the tombs shall hear his voice, and shall come forth; they that have done good, unto the resurrection of life; and they that have done evil unto the resurrection of judgment" (John 5:28,29).

Whereas the first resurrection was to begin taking place during Jesus' earthly ministry, this general resurrection was predicted as being future from that day. This second resurrection is also future from our present day.

The general resurrection — which includes all the dead of all time — is foreshadowed in the Old Testament. Usually, these Old Testament glimpses are rather vague until we come to Daniel.

"And at that time shall Michael stand up, the great prince who standeth for the children of thy people; and there shall be a time of trouble, such as never was since there was a nation even to that same time: and at that time thy people shall be delivered, every one that shall be found written in the book.

"And many of them that sleep in the dust of the earth shall awake, some to everlasting life, and some to shame and everlasting contempt" (Dan. 12:1,2).

We note here that Daniel's prophecy of the resurrection is in perfect harmony with the accounts given in the New Testament. He pictures the resurrection as following a time of great persecution of God's people, and points out that it will bring about a separation of the righteous from the wicked.

Many passages in the New Testament illustrate the fact that the bodily resurrection which is to occur when Christ returns the second time to earth is always, without exception, spoken of in the singular. Martha fixes the singularity and the setting for the resurrection in her conversation with her Lord: "I know that he shall rise again in *the resurrection at the last day*" (John 11:24). And Jesus answered that *he was the resurrection* (vs. 25).

The early church knew and preached but one resurrection. ". . . they taught the people, and proclaimed in Jesus the resurrection from the dead" (Acts 17:18).

When Paul's theology was brought into question by his Jewish enemies he stated specifically, "that there shall be *a* resurrection both of the just and unjust" (Acts 24:15). Paul also stated that this was an Old Testament belief held in common by the Jews, "having hope toward God, *which these also themselves look for,* that there shall be a resurrection both of the just and unjust" (Acts 24:15). It is a reflection upon Paul's use of grammer to say, as some do, that he believed in more than one bodily resurrection. It is also a reflection upon one's theory of inspiration to think that the Holy Spirit would inspire such a statement.

It is difficult to understand how so many persons can ignore these plain verses while they take an obscure passage from Revelation (20:5, 6) and build a doctrine of two or more bodily resurrections upon it. Truly, the letter kills, but the spirit gives life!

Paul condemns those who say the resurrection (singular) is past already (II Tim. 2:18).

If there were more than one physical resurrection, then many of our Scripture passages would not make sense in their present form. It would have been necessary for Paul to have said "I believe in resurrections, one for the just and one for the unjust." Martha would have found it necessary to have specified which resurrection she had

103

in mind when stating that her brother would rise in the last day. And the early church would not have taught "a resurrection," but resurrections (plural). It would not have sufficed to say of the Sadducees, "They say there is no resurrection" (Matt. 22:23). If there were to be more than one bodily resurrection, then it would be said of the Sadducees, "They say there are no resurrections."

Dispensationalists reject the doctrine of one general resurrection of both the righteous and the wicked simply because they are not always dealt with together in Scripture. They argue that since the Bible speaks, for example, of "the resurrection of the just," then there must of necessity be a separate resurrection of the unjust. They also argue that since resurrection chapters such as I Corinthians 15 do not even mention the unsaved dead, then it must follow that the wicked will not be present when the righteous are raised.

First of all, this is to argue from silence which is always poor exegesis. And, more important, these are by no means the only passages of Scripture which deal with only one side of a subject. A similar example may be gained by comparing the four Gospels with reference to the scene at the empty tomb following the resurrection of Christ. Each Gospel writer emphasizes a different fact concerning the angels at the tomb. Matthew 28:2 mentions one angel; Mark 16:5 speaks of a young man; Luke 24:4 refers to two young men; John 20:12 tells of two angels being present.

No problem exists concerning the terms "angels" and "men," for these are used interchangeably elsewhere in Scripture. However, using the same argument used with reference to I Corinthians 15, one could contend — seeing that Matthew and Mark mentioned only one angel (or young man) — the second one was not present at that same time. Therefore, one could contend, these four Gospels do not speak of the same events.

Reason dictates, naturally, that Matthew and Mark saw fit to mention only a part of those present, while Luke and John mentioned the full scene. Reason also dictates this same conclusion with reference to I Corinthians 15 when it is compared with the many other scriptures dealing with the resurrection. Paul, for example, lumps the two groups together in Acts 24:15 and also in II Thessalonians 1 and 2.

In all his epistles Paul deals in practical things, often in answer to questions from the churches. Thus he does not deal specifically with the resurrection of the wicked, because that would not serve his purpose. He deals at length, however, with their punishment, since that would encourage the Christians by letting them know that right will eventually triumph over evil.

Further proof that the righteous and the wicked will be resurrected and judged at the same time lies in the fact that both remain together until the very end of the world (Matt. 13:30, 39, 49, 50). It is difficult to see how the millennialists find one thousand or more years lying between the resurrection of the righteous and that of the wicked. And without this alleged interval, their entire theory goes begging.

When we say the righteous and wicked are to remain together, we do not speak of the souls of the dead, but rather of those persons living when Christ returns. When a Christian dies, his soul goes immediately into the presence of God, while his body returns to the earth (Ecc. 12:7). When a sinner dies, his body also returns to the earth, but his soul goes to a place of conscious torment where it is imprisoned to await the final judgment (Luke 16:19-31; II Peter 2:9). Both will remain in these states of existence until the trump sounds at the end of the world. Then both will be raised together, and judged together, along with all those who remain alive until the second coming.

Having stated that both the righteous and the wicked are to remain together until the second coming, let us look to the Scriptures for proof of this statement.

"Let both grow together *until the harvest:* and in the time of the harvest I will say to the reapers, Gather up first the tares, and bind them in bundles to burn them; but gather the wheat into my barn" (Matt. 13:30, italics added).

"So shall it be *in the end of the world:* the angels shall come forth and sever the wicked from among the righteous, and shall cast them into the furnace of fire: there shall be the weeping and the gnashing of teeth" (Matt. 13:49, 50, italics added).

Paul says, in I Corinthians 15:26, that death will be the last enemy destroyed. Paul goes on to say, beginning with verse 51 of this same chapter, that all Christians will be changed from mortal to immortal *at the last trump.* This resurrection, says Paul, will be the sign that "Death is swallowed up in victory" (vs. 54). Now if the last enemy is to be destroyed at the resurrection of the just, then it is incongruous to picture other enemies still being present one thousand years from that time! Turning to Revelation 20:13-15, we find John the Revelator telling of other things which are to happen at the time death is destroyed: "And death and Hades were cast into the lake of fire. This is the second death, even the lake of fire. And if any was not found written in the book of life, he was cast into the lake of fire."

Both Paul and John are dealing here with the last enemy. Paul says specifically that death will be the last enemy dealt with. Then Paul says that at the time the last enemy *is* dealt with, the saints will be resurrected and rewarded. John, dealing with the destruction of this same last enemy, teaches that at the time the last enemy is dealt with the wicked also will be punished. The reader should note that John describes the second death as taking place *after* Satan has made his final battle against the people of God and that Satan has, in fact, been cast into hell (Rev. 20:10). Note, too, that this final battle which Satan leads takes place *after the millennium* (Rev. 20:7).

The dispensationalist builds his entire millennial thesis on Revelation 20:1-10, just as if the rest of that chapter did not exist. An outline of Revelation 20 reveals that John actually deals with four happenings in their chronological order: (1) the binding of Satan (vss. 1-3), (2) the millennium (vss. 4-6), (3) the battle of Armageddon, fought between Gog and Magog on the one hand and the followers of Christ on the other (vss. 7-10), (4) the final judgment and destruction of the final enemy, death (vss. 11-15).

In speaking of the wheat and the tares (representing the righteous and the wicked) our Lord said, "Let both grow together until the harvest: and in the time of the harvest I will say to the reapers, Gather up first the tares, and bind them in bundles to burn them; but gather the wheat into my barn" (Matt. 13:30).

After the crowd had dispersed, the disciples asked Jesus to explain this parable to them.

"And he answered and said, He that soweth the good seed is the Son of man; and the field is the world; and the good seed, these are the sons of the kingdom; and the tares are the sons of the evil one; and the enemy that sowed them is the devil: and the harvest the end of the world; and the reapers are angels. As therefore the tares are gathered up and burned with fire; so shall it be in the end of the world. The Son of man shall send forth his angels, and they shall gather out of his kingdom all things that cause stumbling, and them that do iniquity, and shall cast them into the furnace of fire: there shall be the weeping and the gnashing of teeth. Then shall the righteous shine forth as the sun in the kingdom of their Father" (Matt. 13:37-43).

An explanation of this passage seems superfluous, owing to the way in which the Lord explained every detail. Yet, many weird misinterpretations have been placed on it. The millennialist teaches that the wicked will be resurrected one thousand years after the resurrection of the just. Yet the Lord teaches (Matt. 13:30) "gather up *first* the tares. . . ."

The Savior said that he spoke of the wicked and the righteous in this present world. He stated specifically—in fact, gave an order to the effect — that the good and bad were to remain together until the end of the world. "And the harvest is the end of the world." "So shall it be in the end of the world." He says that the field spoken of is the world (note that the tares are not in the kingdom of God, but in the world).

Again, it is almost unbelievable that students of the Bible do such violence to these words of our Lord and teach that there will be a millennium between the resurrection of the righteous and that of the wicked. Certainly there can be no interval at all between the resurrection of the two groups if both are to grow side by side until the harvest (which the Bible says is the end of the world). John's single apocalyptic passage in Revelation 20 cannot be allowed to contradict the clear teachings of the entire New Testament. All passages are equally inspired and true, but the plain must interpret the figurative.

In chapter 25 of Matthew the Lord is again recorded as having spoken concerning a separation of the righteous from the wicked. The time is again fixed at the end of the world, i.e., at the second coming of Christ.

"But when the Son of man shall come in his glory, and all the angels with him, then shall he sit on the throne of his glory; and before him shall be gathered all the nations: and he shall separate them one from another, as the shepherd separateth the sheep from the goats. . ." (Matt. 25:31).

We shall deal in detail with this passage when we come to the chapter dealing with the judgment. Suffice it here to say that once again we are reminded that the righteous and the wicked will not be separated until the coming of Christ at the end of the world.

Another evidence that the righteous and the wicked are to remain together until the general resurrection is found in Paul's teaching. Paul definitely teaches that the wicked will be punished at the same time the righteous are rewarded, and he says that both will happen "in that day."

". . . at the revelation of the Lord Jesus from heaven with the angels of his power in flaming fire, rendering vengeance to them that know not God, and to them that obey not the gospel of our Lord Jesus: who shall suffer punishment, even eternal destruction from the face of the Lord and from the glory of his might, when he shall come to be glorified in his saints, and to be marvelled at in all them that believed . . . in that day" (II Thess. 1:7-10).

Paul leaves no doubt or room for speculation as to what he means or as to when it will take place. He says that (1) at the revelation of the Lord Jesus certain things will happen — (a) the wicked will suffer punishment and destruction (compare this with Revelation 20:14), (b) the saints will be rewarded and will escape the persecutions which they now suffer; (2) the time at which the wicked will receive this punishment is "when he [Christ] shall come to be glorified in [with] his saints." If both the rewarding of the saints and the punishment of the wicked are to take place at the same time, i.e., "at the revelation," "when he shall come," "in that day," then it stands to reason that there could not be two separate bodily resurrections, one for the righteous and one for the wicked.

A scriptural conclusion may be based upon the above-mentioned Scripture passages. (A) Death will be the last enemy abolished by Christ; (B) Christians are to be rewarded at the time this last enemy is abolished (I Cor. 15:54); (C) The wicked are to be judged and cast into hell at the time the last enemy is destroyed (Rev. 20:14). Since both events take place at the time of the second death, then both events must of necessity take place at one and the same time. Things equal to the same thing are equal to each other.

The resurrection is to be heralded by the blowing of the last trump (trumpet). This last trump will, in fact, be the signal for many simultaneous events to take place. Certainly it would be "straining at a gnat" to insist on there being more than one *last* trump connected with the end of time. We shall list some of the things to be signaled forth by the blowing of this last trumpet.

1. The last trump will be the signal for Christ to appear (Matt. 24:30,31; I Thess. 4:16).

2. The last trumpet will accompany the earthly phenomena surrounding the second coming of Christ (Matt. 24:29,31).

3. At the sound of the last trump, the wicked will mourn (Matt. 24:30).

4. At the sound of the last trump, the righteous will be raptured (Matt. 24:31; I Cor. 15:51,52; I Thess. 4:16,17).

5. At the last trump, the righteous will be resurrected and given their new bodies (I Cor. 15:51,52).

6. At the last trump the kingdom will be consummated.

7. At the last trump, the wicked will be punished (Rev. 11:15,18). Since all these things happen at one and the same time— and we should note they happen to the righteous and to the wicked simultaneously—it is a contradiction to separate these events by one thousand or more years. This the millennialists attempt to do.


*The Rapture*

"Rapture" is from a Latin word (rapiemur) and portrays a snatching away. This doctrine is based on I Thessalonians 2:1; John 14:3; and Matthew 25:1-13. The "rapture theory" has fallen into ill repute owing to the controversy growing out of the fantastic interpretations of many dispensationalist groups. Most Bible dictionaries do not even list the word.

When looked at sanely and collated with other scriptures, these verses do seem to form a teaching concerning the resurrection of the saints at Jesus' second coming. Perhaps Bible scholars have "thrown the baby out with the bath" in their attempts to completely disassociate themselves from the radicals on this doctrine. For certainly Paul does teach that the saints will be caught up (raptured) to meet the Lord in the air when he comes again. And our Lord himself seems to allude to this in Matthew 25:1-13. There he teaches a lesson concerning the present kingdom of heaven: true believers are to meet Christ on his return. "Behold, the bridegroom! *Come ye forth to meet him* . . . the bridegroom came; and they that were ready went in with him to the marriage feast. . . ." This was based upon a custom of that day to go out and meet a visiting dignitary and to escort him the rest of the way on his journey.

"When a dignitary paid an official visit or *parousia* to a city in Hellenistic times, the action of the leading citizens in going out to meet him and escorting him on the final stage of his journey was called the *apantesis*; it is similarly used in Mt. XXV. 6; Acts XXVIII. 15. So the Lord is pictured as escorted to the earth by His people— those newly raised from death and those who have remained alive. . . ." (Davidson, Stibbs, Kevan, *The New Bible Commentary*, p. 1057).

The rapture of the saints will include every believer from every generation. This means that both Old and New Testament saints will be raised. Then all these, along with all the living saints, will be caught up to meet the Lord in the air. His journey will not cease in mid-air, else he would be meeting the saints instead of the saints meeting him. Actually, the Lord will descend from heaven to earth, and the saints will meet him in mid-air and will escort him the rest of the way.

The rapture will take place immediately after the resurrection and just before the judgment. When the trumpet sounds, things will take place simultaneously. Our Lord will begin his descent to the earth, the brightness of this event will put down Satan, and all the graves will be opened. Instantaneously, the saints who come out of the grave will be given new bodies (I Cor. 15:51,52). The saints who are living at that time will also be given new bodies, then all the saints together will go out to meet the Lord and to escort him to the earth. We are dealing here only with the *bodies* of those who die in the Lord, since their souls will have been in the paradise of God until that instant when they are clothed upon with the new bodies. Christ will bring his (disembodied) saints with him when he comes (I Thess. 3:13; 4:14; Jude 14).

We said that *all* the graves will be opened at the sound of the trump. What then of the unsaved while the saints are being raptured? A number of scriptures concerning them will be fulfilled at that instant. First of all, they will witness the joy of the saints and the rapture. They will be forced to bow the knee and acknowledge that this is of a certainty the Christ (Rom. 14:11; Phil. 2:9-11). This acknowledgment will not, however, bring salvation. For the sound of the trumpet will close the door of salvation. They will see the suffering Servant of the cross reigning now as Judge of the quick and the dead, and they will seek a place of hiding but will find none (Rev. 1:7).

Dispensationalists, and many premillennialists, use the rapture passage in I Thessalonians 4 to argue that the unsaved will not be resurrected at the time the saints are. They base this on Paul's statement in verse 16 that "the dead in Christ shall rise *first*." In this passage Paul is not speaking in relation to the unsaved. The antecedent to the word "first" in this passage is verse 15, wherein Paul had stated that living saints would not be rewarded ahead of those who had died in the Lord. So that what the apostle said was "first" (i.e., before the living Christians are raptured) the souls of those who sleep will be reunited with the living saints; then (only after this has *first* been done) we that are alive, that are left, will together with them be caught up (raptured) in the clouds to meet the Lord in the air.

# IX

## THE JUDGMENT

Judgment is a natural part of God's ongoing plan. Many acts of God, dating back to the fall of man in the Garden of Eden, are classed as judgments by the Bible writers. God has judged national Israel many times. For example, Israel's many captivities are called judgments of God upon his people; and these many judgments culminated in her national destruction by Titus in A.D. 70. The church too has undergone many judgments of God throughout her history. Individual Christians were judged, and justified at the time of their repentance and conversion. Nations too have been judged. In fact, every great catastrophe is looked upon by the Scriptures as God's intervening judgments. Both John the Baptist and Jesus announced that judgment was ushered into the world at the first advent (Matt. 3:10-12; John 12:31).

All these judgments, however, are partial and incomplete. They foreshadow a final day in history when a general judgment will bring history to its close and commence the final state. This final judgment will follow immediately after the second coming, general resurrection, and rapture.

When the last trump sounds, it will be the signal for a number of things to happen. Among them will be the following.

1. The Lord will descend from heaven accompanied by a heavenly host of angels. He will bring with him the souls of all the saints (believers) who have died, from the creation until his second coming. At death these souls left their mortal bodies; the bodies returned to the earth, while the souls went immediately into the presence of God (Ecc. 12:7).

2. All the graves will open. All (both living and dead) will receive new bodies. We must *imply* this concerning the unsaved, for while the Scriptures intimate that they will have bodies matching their evil souls, nothing specific is said concerning the bodies of

the wicked. It seems logical to assume that — since the righteous are to receive immortal bodies to correspond with their immortal souls — the wicked would also have mortal bodies to match their mortal souls. We use the word "mortal" here in the sense of earthly as against the heavenly bodies of saints. Both will remain throughout eternity.

3. All saints, living and dead, having been transformed —the souls of these who have died in the Lord will unite with the new bodies coming out of the grave — will be caught up to meet the Lord in the air. However, his train will not stop in mid-air. Rather, the saints will meet him for the purpose of escorting him to the earth.

4. The Lord, upon coming to the earth "with his saints," will immediately inaugurate the general and final judgment. God the Father will judge through God the Son. The saints, owing to their being joint-heirs with Christ, will assist Christ in the judgment. In other words, our part will be in and through our relationship to our Lord. The glory will be due him.

In outlining these events in numerical order, we, in the words of Paul, "speak as a man." For, after all, God is not limited by time or space. From his perspective all things in the end of time will happen simultaneously. From our finite vantage point, however, it is necessary to record them as though they were to happen in sequence. Even a theological mind such as Paul's was limited by the use of human words. The great apostle came close to describing it though when he said that only the twinkling of the eye would separate the sounding of the trump, the descension, the resurrection, and the rapture (I Cor. 15:51,52).

The final judgment is prefigured many times in the Old Testament. Daniel 7 is one example. It is an indication of the importance of this event when one discovers that the Old Testament devotes its last chapter to this subject. The following passage from Malachi is illustrative.

"For, behold, the day cometh, it burneth as a furnace; and all the proud, and all that work wickedness, shall be stubble; and the day that cometh shall burn them up, saith Jehovah of hosts, that it shall leave them neither root nor branch. But unto you that fear my name shall the sun of righteousness arise with healing in its wings;

113

and ye shall go forth, and gambol as calves of the stall. And ye shall tread down the wicked; for they shall be ashes under the soles of your feet in the day that I make, saith Jehovah of hosts.

"Remember ye the law of Moses my servant, which I commanded unto him in Horeb for all Israel, even statutes and ordinances. Behold, I will send you Elijah the prophet before the great and terrible day of Jehovah come. And he shall turn the heart of the fathers to the children, and the heart of the children to their fathers; lest I come and smite the earth with a curse" (Mal. 4:1-6).

Several enlightening things are taught in this chapter by Malachi concerning the judgment. (1) It is to take place on a single day, (2) both the righteous and the wicked will be present on that day, (3) for the wicked it will be a time of punishment, while it will cause the righteous to rejoice, (4) that day will be preceded by a forerunner who comes in the spirit and power of Elijah, who shall turn the hearts of many Israelites toward repentance so that they would not be overcome by the day of judgment. Those words with reference to Elijah are used in announcing the birth and ministry of John the Baptist, and the New Testament definitely teaches that he fulfilled this prophecy (Matt. 17:13). He was forerunner to the Messiah, he turned the hearts of many Israelites to God, and he announced the coming great day of Jehovah.

While these points are stated in the Old Testament, they are crystalized and enunciated in the New Testament. Jesus stated, "For the Son of man shall come in the glory of his Father with his angels; and then |at that time] he shall reward every man according to his works" (Matt. 16:27).

Every person, from Adam to the last person born on earth, will be present at the judgment. The judgment will not be for the purpose of determining men's destinies, but merely to manifest them. Paul says that all must stand before God (Rom. 14:10; II Cor. 5:10). The saved person will be there to give an account of his deeds since conversion. All things will be manifest, and the righteous will be rewarded according to deeds done in the body. He must give account of his stewardship. This doctrine needs to be returned to by those of us who believe in eternal security! For many have used this precious doctrine — which is clearly taught in the New Testament — as a cloak for license. Christians need to be reminded that we will stand before God, and that we stand to lose rewards even though our salvation is secure (I Cor. 3:13-15). The Christian will never again be judged for salvation; however, he most definitely will be present at the judgment and will be judged to determine the amount of reward he shall receive.

Again, it would seem superfluous indeed to elaborate on the scriptures which deal with the general judgment, except for the fact that so many persons deny that all will stand before God at the same time. Fortunately, we are not left to haggle over prooftexts on this great subject; many complete sections of the Bible deal with the general judgment.


### Matthew Thirteen

We have already used this passage to point up the fact that the righteous and the wicked will remain on the earth together until the trumpet sounds. It is also appropriate, however, in bringing both groups together at the judgment.

Matthew 13:24-30 records a parable of our Lord related to the judgment. Jesus teaches that no separation is to take place until the harvest, which he later explains as being the end of the world. "Let both grow together until the harvest: and in the time of the harvest I will say to the reapers, Gather up first the tares, and bind them in bundles to burn them; but gather the wheat into my barn."

We are not left in doubt as to the meaning of this parable, for the disciples came to the Lord, after the crowds had left, and asked him for an explanation of it. The Lord obliged them, and his interpretation is recorded in verses 26-43. He said that he himself is the sower, the field is the world, and the wheat is the sons of the kingdom (i.e., all believers), the tares are the followers of Satan, the harvest is the end of the world, and the reapers are angels. ". . . so shall it be in the end of the world . . . and shall cast them into the furnace of fire: there shall be the weeping and the gnashing of teeth. Then shall the righteous shine forth as the sun in the kingdom of their Father."

In verses 47-50, the Lord likens the kingdom of heaven to a net used by fishermen. His listeners would immediately visualize what the Master meant by this parable. They had often drawn fishing nets to the shore loaded with good and bad fish. They would also recognize the sorting, casting the bad fish away while keeping the good ones. Let this parable speak for itself.

"Again, the kingdom of heaven is like unto a net, that was cast into the sea, and gathered of every kind: which, when it was filled, they drew up on the beach; and they sat down, and gathered the good into vessels, but the bad they cast away. So shall it be *in the end of the world*; the angels shall come forth, and sever the wicked from among the righteous, and shall cast them into the furnace of fire: there shall be the weeping and the gnashing of teeth" (Matt. 13:47-50, italics added).

### Matthew Twenty-five

Verses 31-46 of this chapter represent another clear teaching concerning the judgment. Rather than quote this long section, we present an outline of it.

(A) The time? "When the Son of man shall come in his glory."

(B) Who will be present? "And before him shall be gathered all the nations."

Dispensationalists attempt to disassociate this scripture from the final judgment of the wicked. They teach that this is a separate judgment "of the nations." This, they say, is not a salvation judgment, but rather a judgment of the Gentile nations to determine which nations will be permitted to remain on earth during the millennium. According to this theory, the Jews will not be present at the judgment in Matthew 25. Nor will it be a judgment of individuals, but rather a judgment of nations.

The dispensationalist prides himself on a literal interpretation of all Scripture. When he comes to this passage, however, he throws all caution to the wind and spiritualizes it completely. "All the nations," he says, actually means "all the nations, *except Israel*." And whereas the Lord says to the wicked, "Depart . . . into eternal fire" (vs. 41), and "And these shall go away into eternal punishment" (vs. 46), what he actually means is, "Depart into an earthly millennium which shall have a limited duration of one thousand years."

116

The dispensationalists' argument rests on their insistence that here we are dealing with nations but not with individuals. Perhaps the best way to refute this argument would be to turn to another passage in this same Gospel, where the Lord is again the speaker, and where he uses this same word. "Go ye therefore, and make disciples of all the nations, baptizing them into the name of the Father and of the Son and of the Holy Spirit: teaching them to observe all things whatsoever I commanded you: and lo, I am with you always, even unto the end of the world" (Matt. 28:19,20).

No Protestant, to our knowledge, would attempt to baptize a *nation*, or even teach a *nation*, or disciple a *nation*. Rather, we would deal with individuals within each nation. And so it will be at the judgment. To say that all the nations will be there is simply another way of saying that every individual will be present. Nations are made up of individuals.

(C) What will happen once the nations are gathered before the throne? "And he shall separate them one from another," placing one group on one side and the other group on the other side. Different destinies will then be assigned to the two groups.

(D) What of the righteous group? "Then shall the King say unto them on his right hand, Come, ye blessed of my Father, inherit the Kingdom prepared for you from the foundation of the world."

(E) What of the wicked? "Then shall he say also unto them on the left hand, Depart from me, ye cursed, into the eternal fire which is prepared for the devil and his angels" (cf. Rev. 20:10,14).

(F) Conclusion? "And these |wicked| shall go away into eternal punishment: but the righteous into eternal life" (vs. 46). Compare John 5:29; Revelation 20:14.

The following statement by Kik is appropriate here: "The average Christian believes that Matthew 25: 31-46 is a picture of the Last Judgment. And he is right. The Premillennialist has to explain this passage away because it does not fit in with his prophetic view. In his interpretation he has to forsake 'literal' interpretation of which he speaks so much. He has to explain that the 'all nations' are not 'all' nations, and that the nations that are there are there only 'representatively.' There is nothing in the passage to indicate this. It is a clear picture of the Last and Universal Judgment" (J. M. Kik, *Matthew Twenty-Four*, p. 94).

### John Five

Having spoken of the first resurrection (vs. 25), or the new birth, the Lord says: "Marvel not at this: for the hour cometh, in which all that are in the tombs shall hear his voice, and shall come forth; they that have done good, unto the resurrection of life; and they that have done evil, unto the resurrection of judgment" (John 5:28,29). This passage speaks for itself, and certainly leaves no room for plural judgments with intervals between.

"And he charged us to preach unto the people, and to testify that this is he who is ordained of God to be the Judge of the living and the dead" (Acts 10:42).

"Inasmuch as he hath appointed a day in which he will judge the world in righteousness by the man whom he hath ordained. . ." (Acts 17:31).

"For the Son of man shall come in the glory of his Father with his angels; and then he shall reward every man according to his works" (Matt. 16:27).

### The Book of Revelation

The book of Revelation makes it clear that the judgment will be of a universal nature. One such picture is in Revelation 11:18. "And the nations were wroth, and thy wrath came, and the time of the dead to be judged, and the time to give their reward to thy servants the prophets, and to the saints, and to them that fear thy name, the small and the great; and to destroy them that destroy the earth."

Here John declares that his vision of the judgment day revealed that the wicked were punished at the same time the righteous were rewarded. John, in fact, completely interchanged the two groups in this passage. He leaves no doubt that both are to take place simultaneously. Otherwise, John reversed the order of the dispensationalists' plurality of judgments by speaking of the wicked before he spoke .of the righteous. Dispensationalists teach that the righteous will be dealt with one thousand and seven years before the wicked are judged. Matthew 13:30 also reverses this order. "Gather first the tares. . . ."

118

In the closing verses (vss. 11-15) of this chapter one finds a most descriptive account of the final universal judgment. John was inspired to place this drama in its chronological order; going before it is recorded the millennium, followed by the loosing of Satan, his final persecution of the church, and his overthrow by Christ. Then John records the general judgment, and follows it with a description of the final state in chapters 21 and 22.

John sees the Lord seated upon a great white throne of judgment. This coincides exactly with the prophecy of Christ recorded in Matthew 25:31, "But when the Son of man shall come in his glory, and all the angels with him, then shall he sit on the throne of his glory." The Lord also prophesied in Matthew 25:32ff that all nations would be brought before him, judged, and sent to their different destinies. John sees this too, and describes it simply, "And I saw the dead, the great and the small, standing before the throne." John saw record books at the judgment, and distinguishes one of these books as "the book of life." Certainly this places the righteous at this event, for it would be nonsensical to state that John was here describing their judgment as having taken place one thousand years earlier! In verse 15, John points out that this book of life was the factor which determined whether or not one was cast into the lake of fire. This lake of fire, John said, is the second death, and he had stated in verse 6 of this chapter that this second death would have no power over those who had had a part in the first resurrection, i.e., those who had been saved.

John speaks in an inclusive sense of "the dead," and says that they are judged "according to their works" as recorded in "the books." This coincides with other clear scriptures such as Matthew 16:27. After this judgment, says John, the second death was pronounced, at which time death and Hades were cast into the lake of fire. We recall Paul's words in I Corinthians 15:26 that death would be the last enemy abolished, and that this abolishment would come to pass when Christians were resurrected. Jesus taught that the saints would not be resurrected until "the last day" (John 6:39, 40, 44, 54).

Throughout the Bible there is pictured a *judgment scene*. This scene recurs time and again as the different inspired writers refer here to the complete scene, there to different facets of the total scene. When all the panoramic pictures are carefully analyzed it is not difficult to piece together a total picture consistent with each different reference.

In the judgment scene, God's power and majesty are always exemplified. One time this will be a reference to God the Father, at another, God the Son. Sometimes both are brought together. This shows the great harmony with which God the Father will judge *through* God the Son.

Viewing the scriptural portrayal of the judgment scene, one is reminded of Isaiah's vision as it is recorded in Isaiah 6. There Isaiah described God as being high and lifted up above all else, his presence filling the entire temple, indicating that all was obscured from view except the majesty of God himself. Descriptive words eluded Isaiah as he attempted to recount his vision of God. Words likewise failed the inspired New Testament writers as they described the judgment scene which will appear in the last day. In John's vision of the majestic judgment scene he said the earth and the heaven fled away from it (Rev. 20:11).

Jesus is pictured in this scene as a trial judge. The judge is seated upon a throne befitting his mien. Jesus predicted this judgment scene in Matthew 25:31-46, and fixed the time at his second coming. "Then shall he sit on the throne of his glory: and before him shall be gathered all the nations" (vs. 31).

Paul mentioned the throne of judgment, referring to it as "the judgment-seat of God" (Rom. 14:10). In II Corinthians 5:10, Paul refers to the throne as "the judgment-seat of Christ." In Paul's Christology, as in the rest of the New Testament, each member of the Trinity was equal. Therefore, their titles could be used interchangeably.

John gives his account of the judgment scene in Revelation 20:11-15. He too sees a throne and speaks of it as "a great white throne." This is John's poetic way of speaking of the sovereignty and holiness of the One seated upon the throne.

There are those who attempt to make seperate and distinct judgments of the above-mentioned thrones and judgment-seats. As they do this, the wish is father to the thought, i.e., they are attempting to justify other preconceived doctrines based on an obscure passage of Scripture.

Historical Christian teaching always has been that these are but different angles of one general judgment scene. The great majority of church fathers, creeds, reformers, and commentaries, could be cited to this effect.

Record books are brought forth in which perfect records have been kept. Perfect justice will therefore prevail. Certainly this is not true of our court cases. But here each person is assured of impartial judgment based upon unquestionable records. John the Revelator points out (Rev. 20:12) that actually two sets of books will be produced at the court scene. The first set of books will condemn every person present as a law breaker. However, the Judge himself has voluntarily undergone punishment in order to pay the penalty demanded by the law! In order to escape the judgment penalty, however, one must have accepted the judge as his substitution. And this acceptance must have been made before court convened. As individuals accepted this free gift their names were entered in the book of life. This book too shall be brought forward at the judgment (Rev. 20:12). "And if any was not found written in the book of life, he was cast into the lake of fire" (Rev. 20:15). Also compare John 5:29 and Matthew 25:46.

The scene under consideration is definitely one of universal judgment. Jesus taught that the repentant would be present with the unrepentant at the judgment. Luke 11:31, 32 records these words: "The queen of the south shall rise up in the judgment with the men of this generation, and shall condemn them: for she came from the ends of the earth to hear the wisdom of Solomon; and behold, a greater than Solomon is here. The men of Nineveh shall stand up in the judgment with this generation, and shall condemn it; for they repented at the preaching of Jonah; and behold, a greater than Jonah is here."

Sodom and Gomorrah (Matt. 10:15) and Tyre and Sidon (Matt. 11:22) all will be present at the judgment along with those to whom the Lord was speaking on that occasion.

One of the clearest pictures of the last judgment found in the Old Testament is in the book of Daniel. Daniel gives an unmistakable picture of a judgment at which both the wicked and the righteous will be present. "And many of them that sleep in the dust of the earth shall awake, some to everlasting life, and some to shame and everlasting contempt" (Dan. 12:2). This agrees completely with the New Testament accounts of the judgment scene which we have already listed (Matt. 25:31-46; Rom. 14:10; II Cor. 5:10; Rev. 20:11-15). It also agrees closely with John 5:28, 29.

Some argue that Daniel did not have in mind a general judgment because he used the word "many" rather than speaking of "all the dead." To this we answer: (1) Daniel has the righteous and the wicked being raised and judged together; this, regardless of the number of persons present, outlaws a time interval between the judgment of the two groups; (2) Owing to progressive revelation, Daniel did not know all the facts concerning the judgment. Certainly he could not give the exact number who would be present. Daniel saw a vision of the last judgment, and he saw that *many* were present. "Many of them that sleep in the dust," in no way contradicts the fact that these "many" represent "all" who sleep in the dust. Jesus filled in the details in John 5:28, 29 by teaching that all that are in the tombs shall come forth.

Daniel records another vision of the judgment in his seventh chapter. There Daniel says that "thousands of thousands" ministered to the judge, and that "ten thousand times ten thousand stood before him" (Dan. 7:10). Most interpreters, considering Daniel's apocalyptic language, do not take this to be a literally exact number. It is more likely that Daniel is attempting to point out that those present at the judgment will be "many."

It is a mistake to apply hyperliteralism to any of the descriptive passages which portray the judgment scene. Here, it would seem obvious, God condescends to the level of our human understanding. He accommodates the word pictures to our understanding. For certainly God does not need literal books in order to know what each person has done. The first century Christians fully understood this language. For they were accustomed to the Bema judgment-seats of earthly judges such as Pilate (Matt. 27:19; John 19:13) and Herod (Acts 12:21), etc. These judgment-seats were elevated and were throne-like. Their elaborateness would depend upon the station of the judge.

Another measure of the universality of the final judgment is the singular way in which it is referred to throughout the Bible. One never reads of "days of judgment," but rather of "the day of judgment," or simply "that day." Christians are to be rewarded "at that day." The unsaved are to be punished "at that day" (Matt. 7:22, 23). The New Testament speaks with finality of "the judgment [singular] of the great day [singular]" in Jude 6.

Paul describes a single day of wrath (Rom. 2:5) during which God will "render to every man according to his works" (1) to one group, eternal life (vs. 7), (2) to another group, wrath and indignation (vs. 8). All this is to happen, says the great Christian theologian, "in the day when God shall judge the secrets of men, according to my gospel, by Jesus Christ" (Rom. 2:6). Compare also John 12:48; I Thessalonians 1:10; I Corinthians 5:5; II Timothy 1:12; 4:1; I John 4:17.

Yes, both the righteous and the wicked are woven by Scripture into the portrait of the judgment scene. The righteous are pictured as joyous, owing to their standing in Christ. The wicked are pictured, always and without exception, as being fearful, bitter, and filled with awe at what they have rejected. As in the case of other doctrines, synonymous terms are used to describe the judgment—such terms as "the judgment seat of Christ," "the great white throne," "the judgment," "the day of judgment," "that day," and so forth. These terms do not portray several different judgments; they are merely different parts of one great mosaic.

# X

## THE FINAL STATE

The second coming of Christ — culminating in the general resurrection and the general judgment — will bring to a close this present age. Then will begin the final state, or, as it is sometimes called, "the eternal state." We prefer the term "final state," because there is a sense in which everything God does is eternal. Actually, the Bible Speaks of only two ages — this world (age) and the world (age) to come (Matt. 12:32; Mark 10:30; Luke 18:30; 20:34; John 8:23).

The final state will differ from the present in that the present age is one of preparation, whereas everything in the final state will be in its completed form. The present age is temporary and thus will come to an end, whereas the final age will last throughout eternity. Time, in its terrestrial form, will no longer exist. Man will no longer be bound by space. Heaven will then extend over all space except the area of hell.

Some things existing in the present world will be ushered into the final state, having been made conformable to the new surroundings of that state. Two examples are the people of God and the kingdom of God. Here, again, however, the transformations will be great between the two worlds. Today, God's people are subject to temptations, sin, and suffering. These will not exist among God's people in the final state. In this life, God's people have immortal souls but they are housed in mortal bodies. Before entering the final state, every believer will receive an immortal body. The kingdom, too, is presently in an incomplete form. Not only are members being added to the kingdom of God daily, but all its members are being constantly shaped and refined in order to rid them of the dross of their Adamic nature. Too, the reign of God in the hearts of his people is taking place amid earthly surroundings. In the world to come, the kingdom of God will be in its consummated and perfected form. God the Son will have turned over the kingdom to God the Father and it will then be marred by no impurities. The full number of the elect — of both Jews and Gentiles — will have come into the kingdom and the number of God's people will be complete. (I believe that, in God's foreknowledge and through his electing, the fullness of the Gentiles will be realized at the exact second the complete number of elected Jews are saved.)

## *Immortality*

Since immortality reaches perfection only in the final state, perhaps a word of definition is in order here. Immortality really has two definitions: (1) the technical theological meaning as listed in the dictionary, and (2) the accepted general meaning with which it usually is associated.

The Winston (Collegiate) Dictionary defines immortality as (1) exemption from death; theological: an everlasting existence with God. (2) time which has unending existence.

The following Greek words are from Strong's Greek lexicon: *aphtharsia*, incorruptibility, generally unending existence; *athanasia*, deathlessness; immortality. Here, again, one can see the two definitions of immortality: (1) incorruptibility, and (2) unending existence.

1. Only a genuine believer in Jesus Christ can lay claim to immortality in its theological sense. For only of the believer, one who has been born from above, may it be said that he is exempt from death and will enjoy an everlasting existence with God.

In order fully to appreciate the technical meaning of immortality as distinguished from its general meaning, one must discover a way in which the saint is eternally different from the sinner. Immortality cannot be taken to mean an exemption from physical death since this comes to the saved as well as to the lost. The bodies of both decay in the earth (Ecc. 12:7). Neither is the Christian different from the non-Christian simply because his soul lives forever, for, we believe, every soul is eternal — the soul of the lost person will spend its eternity in hell, but it will go on existing nonetheless.

In what way, then, is the soul of the Christian uniquely different from that of the person who has never been born again? The

125

physical bodies of both are subject to death, and the souls of both are destined to exist forever. There is one paramount difference between the soul of the twice-born person and that of the unbeliever, i.e., the former is exempt from the second death which is described in Revelation 20:14; this is a spiritual death of the soul. Herein lies true immortality. Every person who reaches the age of accountability will die a first spiritual death, and every such person will also die a natural death — unless he be living when Christ comes (I Cor. 15:51) — but only the genuine believer is immune to the second death.

What makes a person immortal? John gives the answer to this question in the twentieth chapter of the Revelation. "Blessed and holy is he that hath part in the first resurrection: over these the second death hath no power. . ." (Rev. 20:6). Our part in the first resurrection was dealt with in an earlier chapter, and was shown to be the new birth or conversion experience (John 5:24, 25).

A. *Immortality was reflected in the Old Testament.* "But now he is dead, wherefore should I fast? Can I bring him back again? I shall go to him, but he will not return to me" (II Sam. 12:23). David was here speaking of his dead infant son, and we believe that he had in mind more than going to the grave when he stated that he would be reunited with his son.

Job wrestled with the theological question of immortality when he asked the question: "If a man die, shall he live again?" (Job 14:14). He answered his own question in clear terms in the following statement.

"But as for me I know that my Redeemer liveth, and at last he will stand up upon the earth: And after my skin, even this body, is destroyed, then without my flesh shall I see God; Whom I, even I, shall see, on my side, and mine eyes shall behold, and not as a stranger" (Job 19:25-27).

"And many of them that sleep in the dust of the earth shall awake, some to everlasting life, and some to shame and everlasting contempt" (Dan. 12:2). Certainly, Daniel's prediction could not come to pass if physical death ended all.

Although the Old Testament does not deal in detail with life after death, we certainly are given glimpses of it through God's

126

inspired prophets. One sees progressive revelation at work as one turns to the fuller light of the New Testament.

B. *Jesus' resurrection proved the doctrine of immortality.* Much of Paul's theology is based on the fact of Jesus' bodily resurrection. "If Christ be not risen. . .," says this great theologian, then all would be in vain — our faith, our preaching, our hope of a hereafter. But —and here one can almost hear Paul shouting the Hallelujah Chorus — exclaims Paul, Christ *is risen* and has become the first-fruits of those Christians of all ages who sleep the sleep of death. Because of this fact, each believer, in his own order, shall be raised and given a glorified body like that of the risen Christ.

Our Lord himself based the future of his followers on the fact that the sepulchre could not hold him. ". . . because I live, ye shall live also" (John 14:19).

C. *Immortality for the individual Christian begins at the new birth.* Immortality, like sanctification, is both an act and a process. He who has the Son *has* life, and shall never come into condemnation. To repent of sin and be genuinely converted is to become a recipient of eternal life. It is to pass instantly from spiritual death to spiritual life. "Being therefore justified by faith, we have peace with God through our Lord Jesus Christ; through whom also we have had our access by faith into his grace wherein we stand" (Rom. 5:1). "There is therefore *now* no condemnation to them that are in Christ Jesus" (Rom. 8:1).

The preceding, and many similar passages, refer to the *act* of immortality. There is also the *process* through which immortality travels to its completion. There is a definite tension between what the immortal person is and what he is to become. Immortality is like money in the bank — and the check is drawn on a bank which cannot fail — yet, the Christian will not cash the check until the second coming of Christ. The gift of the Holy Spirit, at conversion, is spoken of as a down payment on a much fuller reward which is to come.

"Now he that established us with you in Christ, and anointed us, is God; who also sealed us, and gave us the earnest of the Spirit in our hearts" (II Cor. 1:21, 22).

"Now he that wrought us for this very thing is God, who gave unto us the earnest of the Spirit" (II Cor. 5:5).

127

".  .  . in whom, having also believed, ye were sealed with the Holy Spirit of promise, which is an earnest of our inheritance, unto the redemption of God's own possession, unto the praise of his glory" (Eph. 1:13, 14).

Even though the apostle Paul possessed, and taught, a present-tense salvation (immortality) he also taught that this was merely a shadow or foretaste of the joy of the salvation which is to be the lot of the Christian in the final state. "If we have only hoped in Christ in this life, we are of all men most pitiable" (I Cor. 15:19).

D. *Immortality is enhanced at physical death.* The intermediate state — although this is not the final state — is, for the Christian, a place of conscious bliss in the presence of the Savior. Jesus said to the believing thief on the cross: ".  .  . today shalt thou be with me in Paradise" (Luke 23:43). Jesus taught that, while life still went on in the earth, Lazarus, the beggar, died and went immediately into Paradise (Abraham's bosom) (Luke 16:22).

Paul did not expect to receive his final rewards until the day of the Lord. However, he was inspired to teach that physical death would represent an immediate improvement in his state of immortality.

"For me to live is Christ, and to die is gain. .  .  . But I am in a strait betwixt the two, having the desire to depart and be with Christ; for it is very far better; yet to abide in the flesh is more needful for your sake" (Phil. 1:21-24).

E. *Immortality will be consummated at the second coming.* Much language of the Bible will be fully realized only in the final state. Nothing this side of eternity completely satisfies the meaning of prophecies concerning the lion lying down with the lamb, perfect peace, perfect laws, every knee bowing at the name of Christ, and the like.

"The Second Advent of Christ will coincide with the final and complete manifestation of the kingdom, when every knee will bow in His name and every tongue confess Him as Lord (Phil. 2:10f), when God's will is to be done on earth as it is done in heaven (Matt. 6:10). At Christ's first coming the age to come invaded this present age; at His second coming the age to come will have altogether superseded this present age. Between the two comings the two ages overlap; Christians live temporally in this present age while spiritually they belong to the heavenly kingdom and enjoy the life of the age to come. Biblical eschatology is largely, but not completely, "realized"; there still remains a future element, to become actual at the Second Advent, the *parousia*. . ." (F. F. Bruce, *The Book of the Acts, The New International Commentary on The New Testament,* p. 35).

An immortal soul is incomplete without a body. Paul teaches in Romans 8:23 that those who have the firstfruits of the Spirit, i.e., Christians, long for a future redemption of their bodies. Thus the saved soul is in an incomplete state until then. In this life, our souls remain in corruptible bodies; when we depart this life — even though our souls go immediately into the presence of Jesus — they are disembodied souls.

". . . the creation itself also shall be delivered from the bondage of corruption into the liberty of the glory of the children of God. For we know that the whole creation groaneth and travaileth in pain together until now. And not only so, but ourselves also, who have the firstfruits of the Spirit, even we ourselves groan within ourselves, waiting for our adoption, to wit, the redemption of our body" (Rom. 8:21-23).

A comparison of other Scripture passages shows that the new body will not be received until the second advent of Jesus.

"For our citizenship is in heaven; whence also we wait for a Saviour, the Lord Jesus Christ: who shall fashion anew the body of our humiliation, that it may be conformed to the body of his glory, according to the working whereby he is able even to subject all things unto himself" (Phil. 3:20, 21).

"When Christ, who is our life, shall be manifested, then shall ye also with him be manifested in glory" (Col. 3:4).

"For as in Adam all die, so also in Christ shall all be made alive. But each in his own order: Christ the firstfruits; then they that are Christ's, at his coming" (I Cor. 15:22, 23).

Only in the final state shall the believer enjoy the full benefits of immortality. Only then shall he cease to view the things of God through an imperfect mirror (I Cor. 13:12). "For this corruptible *must* put on incorruption, and this mortal *must* put on immortality" (I Cor. 15:53, italics added).

2. Although, as stated earlier, the unbeliever does not possess immortality in its strictest theological sense, he does, nonetheless, possess it in its secondary sense, i.e., an unending existence. The soul of the wicked will suffer the second death and will be condemned to spend its eternity separated from God. But it will not cease to exist or to be conscious (Ecc.12:7). The eternity of the wicked is just as long as that of the saint. If there is an eternal heaven for the saved there is a hell of equal duration for the unsaved. Jesus spoke of hell as an actual place where their worm dieth not and the fire is not quenched.

A. *The wicked are condemned already.* Jesus did not come into the world (primarily) for the purpose of judging sinners. His primary mission was to seek and to save the lost. However, those who reject his offer of free salvation thereby seal their own judgment. Unless and until a person comes under the shed blood of Christ, the wrath of God abides on that person.

"He that believeth on him is not judged: he that believeth not hath been judged already, because he hath not believed on the name of the only begotten Son of God. And this is the judgment, that the light is come into the world, and men loved the darkness rather than the light; for their works were evil" (John 3:18, 19).

B. *Their condition worsens at physical death.* The Scriptures make crystal clear the fact that the soul of the wicked, at death, enters into a state of conscious torment. Jesus contrasted for us the intermediate state of the wicked as over against that of the righteous in Luke 16.

". . . and the rich man also died, and was buried. And in Hades he lifted up his eyes, being in torments, and seeth Abraham afar off, and Lazarus in his bosom. And he cried and said, Father Abraham, have mercy on me, and send Lazarus, that he may dip the tip of his finger in water, and cool my tongue; for I am in anguish in this flame. But Abraham said, Son remember that thou in thy lifetime receivedst thy good things, and Lazarus in like manner evil things: But now here he is comforted, and thou art in anguish. And besides all this, between us and you there is a great gulf fixed, that they that would pass from hence to you may not be able, and that none may cross over from thence to us" (Luke 16:22-26).

130

"The Lord knoweth how to deliver the godly out of temptation and to keep the unrighteous under punishment unto the day of judgment" (II Peter 2:9).

C. *The condemnation of the wicked will be finalized at the second coming.* "And to you that are afflicted rest with us, at the revelation of the Lord from heaven with the angels of his power in flaming fire, rendering vengeance to them that know not God, and to them that obey not the gospel of our Lord Jesus: who shall suffer punishment, even eternal destruction from the face of the Lord and from the glory of his might, when he shall come to be glorified in his saints, and to be marvelled at in all them that believed (because our testimony unto you was believed) in that day" (II Thess. 1:7-10). Also compare Matthew 25:31,41,46 and Revelation 20:11-15.

"He that rejecteth me, and receiveth not my sayings, hath one that judgeth him: the word that I spake, the same shall judge him in the last day" (John 12:48).

We noted earlier that the wicked, at death, go immediately into torment (Luke 16:22ff). Here we see that their full punishment does not begin until the end of the world. What of their intermediate state? A collation of scriptures would seem to indicate that their punishment, which begins at death, will be compounded at the judgment.

"The Lord knoweth how to deliver the godly out of temptation, and to keep the unrighteous under punishment unto the day of judgment" (II Peter 2:9).

"And angels that kept not their own principality, but left their proper habitation, he hath kept in everlasting bonds under darkness unto the judgment of the great day" (Jude 6).

The intermediate state of the wicked is to his final state what the prison death cell is to the gas chamber. The person in the death cell can see the chamber and suffers the mental torment of expectation. But the worst of his punishment is ahead. However, this is merely an earthly analogy and we dare not carry it to extremes. For example, the pain of the gas chamber is short-lived while the pain of hell will continue forever.

131

## The Final State of the Earth

In the early chapters of Genesis one reads the account of Paradise lost. The earth was corrupted by sin; and we believe that the universal flood, which resulted from man's disobedience, changed the very appearance of God's created world. The closing chapters of the Revelation record Paradise regained.

The regeneration of the world was predicted in the Old Testament. The following passages will serve as examples.

"Of old didst thou lay the foundation of the earth; and the heavens are the work of thy hands. They shall perish, but thou shalt endure; yea, all of them shall wax old like a garment; as a vesture shalt thou change them, and they shall be changed" (Psalm 102:25, 26).

"For, behold, I create new heavens and a new earth; and the former things shall not be remembered, nor come into mind" (Isa. 65:17).

Naturally, these predictions were given in the language of that day. The following quotation, concerning fulfillment, is apropos.

"In form," writes Dr. Albertus Pieters, "prediction and fulfillment are diverse, in essence they are the same. This principle applies to the New Testament no less than the Old. We are promised eternal life in heaven, and to make us realize it we read of many mansions, of white raiment, of harps of gold, of a river of life to quench our thirst, of the fruit of the tree of life for food, of medicinal leaves of healing, of golden streets, and a heavenly city that has a wall and twelve gates. Such things are needed to convey to us the purpose of God to supply every need and to cause us to dwell in perfect peace and safety, but in what form the reality will be enjoyed we cannot tell, because we do not know what our situation and needs will be in the disembodied state, or after the soul has been reunited to the body in resurrection. Only we do know that whatever such things would mean to us now, of abundant provision, perfect security and glorious existence, shall be fulfilled, and more than fulfilled." (Quoted from "Prophetic Studies" by Dr. John Wilmot, in the July 25, 1963 issue of *The Gospel Witness*. p. 7.)

The following passages are examples of New Testament predictions with reference to the final state of the earth.

"For the creation was subjected to vanity, not of its own will, but by reason of him who subjected it, in hope that the creation itself also shall be delivered from the bondage of corruption into the liberty of the glory of the children of God" (Rom. 8:20, 21).

"But the day of the Lord will come as a thief; in the which the heavens shall pass away with a great noise, and the elements shall be dissolved with fervent heat, and the earth and the works that are therein shall be burned up. Seeing that these things are thus all to be dissolved, what manner of persons ought ye to be in all holy living and godliness, looking for and earnestly desiring the coming of the day of God, by reason of which the heavens being on fire shall be dissolved, and the elements shall melt with fervent heat? But, according to his promise, we look for new heavens and a new earth, wherein dwelleth righteousness" (II Peter 3:10-13).

"And I saw a new heaven and a new earth: for the first heaven and the first earth are passed away; and the sea is no more" (Rev. 21:1).

John devotes the last two chapters of the Revelation to an apocalyptic description of the final state. Here we see Paradise regained.

In all probability, the scriptural references to the destruction of the present world and the setting up of a new one should be interpreted in the same manner as those which refer to the regeneration of the individual Christians. Although Paul speaks of the believer as a new creation in Christ and says that old things "are passed away," we know that the old self was not annihilated. But the change was so radical that Paul could speak in terms of a destruction of the old and the birth of a completely new person.

So it will be, we suspect, with the universe at the second coming of Christ. We believe that the present earth will be completely renovated, but not annihilated.

"What a mighty, all-comprehensive, and blessed change that will be! We need not proceed on the assumption that the old creation will be entirely annihilated, though the form of it and the conditions prevailing in it will undergo a radical change. The imperfections of the present universe, which resulted from sin, will be removed; heaven and earth will again appear in their pristine beauty. The present world is full of unrighteousness. People are clamoring for righteousness in every domain: in social and civic life, in industry and business, in commercial and international relations, and even in the religious sphere. How different that will be in the new creation! It will be a world characterized by holiness and righteousness. The bitter cries of dissatisfaction and injustice will be replaced by songs of thanksgiving and paeans of victory. It will be a fit dwelling place for the glorified Christ and his redeemed and glorified Church" (L. Berkhof, *The Second Coming of Christ,* p. 85).

"It should be made clear, however, that annihilation of the earth is not clearly taught in the Scriptures. The word parerchomai which is translated 'pass away' does not mean annihilate. Culver says, 'The meaning is rather to pass from one position in time or space to another. And even granting the most destructive ideas as the meaning of luthestai (be dissolved) and katakaesetai (be burned up, if we adopt the Textus Receptus), the words certainly do not describe annihilation.' Peter speaks of the two world judgments: one by water, the Flood, in which the world 'perished' but was obviously not annihilated; and one by fire, in which the world shall be burned up, but not necessarily annihilated" (Paul Erb, *The Alpha and the Omega,* p. 119).


### Christ's Second Coming is the Pivotal Point

The present world will come to an end and the final state will begin at the second coming of Christ. In fact, many events will synchronize at the second advent. Both the general resurrection and the general judgment will take place then, the saints will be raptured and rewarded, the wicked will be judged, the earth will be cleansed, Satan will be put down, and the perfected kingdom will be turned over to God the Father by God the Son. Is it any wonder that Paul calls the second coming the Blessed Hope of the Christian?

The present age, which lies between the incarnation and the second coming, might be compared to a woman in pangs of childbirth. The delivery has begun. Each day, each event, sees the birth nearing completion. Paul indeed uses this illustration in Romans 8:23. This could be taken to represent the individual believer, or the church, or the kingdom of God. There is a tension between what we already are and what God has in store for us following the harvest. The

Christian has eternal life; he is a member of the kingdom of God; his citizenship already is in heaven. Yet, he has not possessed his possessions.

At the second coming the tension which now exists between what we are, on the one hand, and fulfilled immortality, on the other, will be removed. In the final state, our bodies will have been made amenable to Spirit rule (Rom. 8:11). The earth will have been cleansed and made suitable for spiritual living. What now is true in heaven will then be true of all of creation. God's will then truly will be done on earth as it is in heaven.

This is not to say that everything for the Christian is "pie-in-the-sky-bye-and-bye." Quite the contrary is true. Eternity broke into history at the incarnation. Man has already been initiated into the kingdom of God and has tasted the joys of heaven (Col. 1:13). The kingdom of God is used synonymously with eternal life in the Gospels. However, this is only a foretaste of that which God has in store for his own. The parousia will mark a dividing line between what we are in miniature as compared with the full enjoyment of immortality.

## SUMMARY AND CONCLUSION

Amillennialism is as old as the Christian church itself. Contrary to its critics, amillennialism is not an innovation among modern theologians. Church fathers such as Origen and Augustine struck out against chiliastic teachings in their days. In fact, chiliasm (millennialism) lay dormant from Augustine's time until its revival in the nineteenth century.

Every well-known Protestant reformer held amillennial beliefs. These beliefs overstep denominational lines. It is a crass misrepresentation of facts to say, as some critics do say, that amillennialism grew out of Roman Catholicism, or liberalism, or covenant theology.

Many of the church's outstanding evangelists, theologians, and commentators have believed amillennial doctrine. Most, if not all, of the historic confessions and creeds contain this teaching. However, while amillenarians can claim outstanding predecessors, their ultimate authority is the Bible. Amillenarians accept the entire Bible as the Spirit-breathed, infallible Word of God.

Negatively speaking, amillenarians reject a literal, earthly, materialistic millennium as being contrary to the clear teachings of Scripture. Positively, however, they believe in the millennium of Revelation twenty. Interpreting this single obscure passage by the myriad clear teachings in the Bible, amillenarians look on the millennium as being the interadvent period. In other words, the millennium is a present reality. It was ushered in by Christ's first advent and will be succeeded by the final (eternal) state at his second coming.

Amillenarians feel that the alleged earthly millennium taught by all millenarians—be they postmillenarian or premillenarian—is arrived at only through a hyperliteral interpretation of obscure passages of Scripture. They feel that far too much is based on the one passage in Revelation twenty (20:1-6) for at least two reasons: first, this is the only mention in the entire Bible of a one thousand year reign, and this one passage is couched in a book of the Bible which is known to be written in figurative and symbolical language; second, obscure passages of Scripture must always be governed by the clear passages, and clear passages just will not allow the interpretation placed on Revelation 20:1-6 by millenarians.

Dr. George Ladd, himself a premillenarian, admits that his cause rests on the figurative language of the book of Revelation. The following statements are from Ladd's book, *Crucial Questions About the Kingdom of God.*

"It must be granted that the one book in the New Testament which teaches the millennial interregnum is the Apocalypse" (p. 170).

"In the Revelation . . . for the first time, Scripture teaches that there is to be an interregnum, a temporal, earthly kingdom, which precedes the final eternal age to come of the new heavens and the new earth" (p. 182).

"In the Revelation . . . for the first time, it is clear that the resurrection is to take place in two stages; a resurrection of the saved before the millennium and a resurrection of the unsaved at its termination" (pp. 182-83).

These quotations are used here because they so graphically show the basis of millenarian thought which is rejected by the amillenarian. More and more scholars are coming to see, with Dr. Ladd, that the alleged earthly interregnum between this age and the final state rests squarely on an interpretation of Revelation 20:1-6. The amillenarian further states that this belief rests on a *hyperliteral* interpretation of this lone passage.

Conservative amillenarians interpret Scripture in the grammatical-historical literal method. Their axiom is "literal where possible." All schools of thought spiritualize some passages of Scripture, so that amillenarians are no different from any other group in this respect. They spiritualize given passages where they feel a literal interpretation does violence to the inspired writer's meaning. It is definitely untrue, however, to say with Dr. Walvoord that amillenarians take any whole section of the Scriptures spiritually. The amillenarian approach to each verse of the Bible is "literal where possible."

There are no literalists! Even those groups who claim to be literalists are known to spiritualize many passages of Scripture whenever a literal interpretation would disprove their presuppositions.

137

We gave illustrations of this earlier in this book. The question, then, is not whether or not Scripture is to be spiritualized, but which passages. And does our spiritual interpretation of any given passage square with sound principles of hermeneutics?

Amillenarians believe God has one eternal plan of salvation. Old Testament saints were saved by looking forward to the cross of Christ, while all others who are saved—or who ever will be saved—come under the same plan of redemption which is based on the finished work of Calvary. Salvation has never been by the works of the law. Nor will it ever be. All men, Jew and Gentile alike, stand in need of salvation. Salvation is to sin what medical cure is to disease. Salvation is a complete package—beginning with our regeneration and ending in our complete glorification in heaven.

Amillenarians believe in two aspects of the one true church—the invisible and the visible. The church is clearly mentioned in both testaments. National Israel was the type while the church is the antitype. The faithful remnant within Israel was the true church of the Old Testament. Old Testament prophecies concerning the new-covenant church were naturally clothed in the language of the day in which the prophet lived. Their fulfillments came about, however, in the language and framework of the generations in which they were fulfilled.

Jesus ushered in the new manifestation of the church. Taking the faithful remnant of national Israel as a nucleus, he built his church upon the foundation of the prophets and apostles. Christ himself is the chief cornerstone. The church is the body of Christ, and is therefore the very fullness of God (Eph. 1:23).

All promises to national Israel have been either fulfilled or invalidated through unbelief. Any unfulfilled spiritual promises will be fulfilled through the church, and will therefore involve all the saved—Jew and Gentile. Some amillenarians believe there will be a future regathering of national Israel. Those who hold this belief, however, believe this regathering will take place within the history of this present age, and that this remnant will be gathered into the Christian church. Amillenarians reject any idea of separate destinies for Israel and the church.

According to amillenarian doctrine, two ages are set forth in the Bible. These are the present age and the age to come, or the final state. The Scriptures neither teach nor allow an interregnum between these two ages. The first advent ushered in the last days. Jesus set eschatology in motion. He bound Satan. "The millennium," although it is not a biblical term, is a poetic way of referring to this present age. The millennium commenced at the first advent and will be consummated at the second coming of Christ. During this millennial age, Christ is reigning in the hearts of his people. Christ has overcome Satan and the world.

Satan, though bound, still goes about like a roaring lion seeking whom he may devour. The chain with which he is bound is a long one, allowing him much freedom of movement. Amillenarians find no contradiction between the fact that Satan is "bound," yet at the same time able to create havoc on the earth. Revelation 20 merely states that Satan is bound in one aspect of his power: "that he should deceive the nations no more." John neither says nor implies that Satan is immobilized. Many modern gangland bosses have exercised their influence while they themselves were incarcerated.

Satan will be loosed near the end of time, and will lead a final, bitter assault against the church. The church will go through the tribulation. This tribulation has in fact already begun, but will grow progressively worse until the man of sin himself is released. Christ's second coming will put down the man of sin (Satan) and will cast him into the lake of fire, where he will spend eternity with all his followers.

In the last day (singular) of these last days (plural) the second coming of Christ will bring history to its close and usher in the final state. We have said that Jesus set eschatology in motion at his first advent. The things commenced there will be consummated at his second coming.

The second coming will not be extended over a long period of time. It will be a singular, cataclysmic event. Christ *himself* will come in a literal, visible, bodily manner and every eye will behold him. Every knee will bow and every tongue confess that he is Lord. However, this forced confession will not bring salvation to those who, up to that time, have disbelieved.

At the second advent, several things will happen more or less simultaneously. Christ will descend from heaven with his holy angels, bringing with him the souls of those who now sleep in him. All the graves will be opened. All the saved, both in and out of the grave, will be given resurrected bodies. They then will be raptured (caught

139

up) to meet the Lord in the air—for the purpose of escorting him to the earth, where the judgment will immediately take place. The wicked, also raised at that time, will cry for the rocks to fall on them; they will seek death but not find it.

The resurrection and rapture will be followed by the general judgment. The great separation of Matthew 25 will take place. Believers will be judged, but only to ascertain their rewards. Because of their part in the first resurrection (the new birth), the second death can have no power over them. The wicked, Jew and Gentile alike, will be judged and cast into the lake of fire—which is the second death.

In this book, the terms "eternal state" and "final state" have been used interchangeably. The first term was used throughout the first nine chapters, since most readers probably would find it more familiar than the latter term, used and explained in chapter 10. The present writer feels that many other scriptural terms — such as the "new heaven and the new earth," the "age to come," etc — are also synonyms for the final state. I base this belief on the axiom that things equal to the same thing are equal to each other.

The earth will also be "judged," cleansed, and completely renovated. Paradise lost will become Paradise regained. God the Son will turn the perfected kingdom over to God the Father so that God may be all in all. Christ will not lose in this exchange, seeing that he is an equal member of the Godhead. Because of their standing in Christ, the saints will reign throughout eternity in the new heaven and new earth. Temporal space barriers will have disappeared, leaving only heaven and hell. In one sense of the word, we will reign on the earth, because heaven will then encompass the cleansed earth. However, this reign will not last a mere thousand years; it will have no end.

Even so, come, Lord Jesus.

# BIBLIOGRAPHY

ALLIS, O. T. *Prophecy and the Church*. Philadelphia: Presbyterian and Reformed Publishing Company, 1945.

BARROW, E. R. *Companion to the Bible*. New York: The American Tract Society, 1867.

BERKHOF, L. *The Second Coming of Christ*. Grand Rapids: Wm. B. Eerdmans Publishing Company, 1953.

————. *Systematic Theology*. Grand Rapids: Wm. B. Eerdmans Publishing Company, 1953.

BIRD, T. C. *Drama of the Apocalypse*. Boston: Roxburgh Publishing Company, 1912.

BOETTNER, LORAINE. *The Millennium*. Philadelphia: Presbyterian and Reformed Publishing Company, 1957.

BRIGHT, JOHN. *The Kingdom of God*. New York: Abingdon Press, 1953.

BUIS, HARRY. *A Simplified Commentary on the Book of Revelation*. Philadelphia: Presbyterian and Reformed Publishing Company, 1960.

CHAFER, L. S. *Dispensationalism*. Dallas: Dallas Seminary Press, 1951.

————. *The Kingdom in History and Prophecy*. Chicago: Fleming H. Revell, 1915.

————. *Systematic Theology*. Dallas: Dallas Seminary Press, 1948.

CHAMBERLAIN, W. D. *The Church Faces the Isms*. (Edited by Arnold Black Rhodes.) New York: Abingdon Press, 1958.

COX, W. E. *An Examination of Dispensationalism*. Philadelphia: Presbyterian and Reformed Publishing Company, 1963.

————. *Biblical Studies in Final Things*. Philadelphia: Presbyterian and Reformed Publishing Company, 1966.

————. *In These Last Days*. Philadelphia: Presbyterian and Reformed Publishing Company, 1964.

————. *The Millennium*. Philadelphia: Presbyterian and Reformed Publishing Company, 1964.

————. *The New-Covenant Israel*. Philadelphia: Presbyterian and Reformed Publishing Company, 1963.

DODD, C. H. *The Parables of the Kingdom*. New York: Charles Scribner's Sons, 1961.

DOUTY, NORMAN F. *Has Christ's Return Two Stages?* New York: Pageant Press, Inc., 1956.

ERB, PAUL. *The Alpha and the Omega*. Scottdale, Pa.: Herald Press, 1955.

GAEBELEIN, A. C. *The Prophet Daniel*. Grand Rapids: Kregel Publications, n.d.

GORDON, S. D. *Quiet Talks About Jesus*. Chicago: Fleming H. Revell, 1906.

HALLEY, H. H. *Halley's Bible Handbook*. Grand Rapids: Zondervan Publishing Company, 1962.

141

HAMILTON, F. E. *The Basis of Millennial Faith*. Grand Rapids: Wm. B. Eerdmans Publishing Company, 1955.

HENDRICKSEN, WILLIAM. *More Than Conquerors*. Grand Rapids: Baker Book House, 1949.

————. *Three Lectures on the Book of Revelation*. Grand Rapids: Zondervan Publishing Company, 1949.

HENRY, CARL F. H. *The Uneasy Conscience of Modern Fundamentalism*. Grand Rapids: Wm. B. Eerdmans Publishing Company, 1947.

HOBBS, H. H., *Fundamentals of Our Faith*. Nashville: Broadman Press, 1960.

HODGES, JESSE WILSON. *Christ's Kingdom and Coming*. Grand Rapids: Wm. B. Eerdmans Publishing Company, 1957.

HUGHES, ARCHIBALD. *New Heaven and New Earth*. Philadelphia: Presbyterian and Reformed Publishing Company, 1957.

JOHNSTON, GEORGE. *The Doctrine of the Church in the New Testament*. New York: Cambridge University Press, 1943.

KIK, J. M. *Matthew XXIV*. Philadelphia: Presbyterian and Reformed Publishing Company, 1948.

————. *Revelation XX*. Philadelphia: Presbyterian and Reformed Publishing Company, 1955.

LADD, G. E. *The Blessed Hope*. Grand Rapids: Wm. B. Eerdmans Publishing Company, 1956.

————. *Crucial Questions About the Kingdom of God*. Grand Rapids: Wm. B. Eerdmans Publishing Company, 1952.

LARKIN, CLARENCE. *Dispensational Truth*. Philadelphia: Rev. Clarence Larkin, Est. 1920.

MASSELINK, WILLIAM. *Why Thousand Years?* Grand Rapids: Wm. B. Eerdmans Publishing Company, 1930.

MAURO, PHILIP. *The Gospel of the Kingdom*. Boston: Hamilton Bros., 1928.

————. *The Seventy Weeks and the Great Tribulation*. Swengel, Pennsylvania: Bible Truth Depot, 1944.

McCALL, DUKE K. (ed.). *What Is the Church?* Nashville: Broadman Press, 1958.

McDOWELL, E. A. *The Meaning and Message of the Book of Revelation*. Nashville: Broadman Press, 1951.

MORGAN, G. CAMPBELL. *Studies in the Prophecy of Jeremiah*. Chicago: Fleming H. Revell, 1931.

MULLINS, E. Y. *The Christian Religion in Its Doctrinal Expression*. Nashville: The Sunday School Board of the Southern Baptist Convention, 1917.

MURRAY, G. L. *Millennial Studies*. Grand Rapids: Eerdmans Publishing Company, 1948.

PIETERS, ALBERTUS. "A Candid Examination of the Scofield Bible" (pamphlet). Swengel, Penn.: Bible Truth Depot, n.d.

————. *The Seed of Abraham*. Grand Rapids: Wm. B. Eerdmans Publishing Company, 1950.

QUISTORP, HEINRICH. *Calvin's Doctrine of the Last Things*. Richmond: John Knox Press, 1955.

REESE, ALEXANDER. *The Approaching Advent of Christ*. London: Marshall, Morgan and Scott, 1937.

RIDDERBOS, HERMAN N. *When the Time Had Fully Come, Studies in New Testament Theology*. Grand Rapids: Wm. B. Eerdmans Publishing Company, 1957.

ROBINSON, H. W. *The History of Israel.* London: Duckworth, 1938.

SCOFIELD, C. I. *The Scofield Reference Bible.* London: Oxford Press, 1909.

———. *What Do the Prophets Say?* Philadelphia: The Sunday School Times, 1916.

STRONG, A. H. *Outlines of Systematic Theology.* Philadelphia: Judson Press, 1942.

SUMMERS, RAY. *The Life Beyond.* Nashville: Broadman Press, 1959.

———. *Worthy Is the Lamb.* Nashville: Broadman Press, 1951.

VOS, GEERHARDUS. *The Pauline Eschatology.* Princeton: Princeton University Press, 1930.

WALVOORD, JOHN. *The Millennial Kingdom.* Findley, Ohio: Dunham Publishing Company, 1959.

WARFIELD, B. B. *Biblical and Theological Studies.* Philadelphia: Presbyterian and Reformed Publishing Company, 1952.

———. "The Millennium and the Apocalypse," *Biblical Doctrines.* New York: Oxford University Press, 1929.

ZORN, RAYMOND O. *Church and Kingdom.* Philadelphia: Presbyterian and Reformed Publishing Company, 1962.

## COMMENTARIES

BRUCE, F. F. *The Book of Acts.* Grand Rapids: Wm. B. Eerdmans Publishing Company, 1955.

CLARKE, ADAM. *Clarke's Commentary.* New York: Abingdon-Cokesbury Press, n.d.

DAVIDSON, F. (ed.). *The New Bible Commentary.* Grand Rapids: Eerdmans Publishing Company, 1953.

DOUGLAS, J. D. *The New Bible Dictionary.* Grand Rapids: Wm. B. Eerdmans Publishing Company, 1962.

MILLER, D. M. *The Topical Bible Concordance.* London: Lutterworth Press, 1950.

STRONG, JAMES. "Greek Dictionary of the New Testament," *Strong's Exhaustive Concordance of the Bible.* New York: Abingdon-Cokesbury Press, 1890.

TERRY, MILTON S. *Biblical Hermeneutics.* (Vol. II). New York: Methodist Book Concern, 1911.

## PERIODICALS

PIETERS, ALBERTUS. "Darbyism vs. the Historical Faith," *Calvin Forum*, II (May, 1936), 225-28.

———. *The Leader*, September, 1934.

VOS, J. G. *Blue Banner Faith and Life*, Oct.-Dec., 1949.

WALVOORD, JOHN. *Bibliotheca Sacra*, Jan.-Mar., 1951.

# DATE DUE